GW01326067

When learning becomes your enemy:
the relationship between education, spiritual dissent and economics

by **Clive Erricker**

Educational Heretics Press

Published 2002 by Educational Heretics Press
113 Arundel Drive, Bramcote Hills, Nottingham NG9 3FQ

British Cataloguing in Publication Data

Erricker, Clive
      When learning becomes your enemy:
      the relationship between education, spiritual
      dissent and economics
      1.Education – Aims and objectives 2.Politics and
      education 3.Education – Economic aspects
      4.Democracy
      I.Title
      370.1

    ISBN   1-900219-25-5

Design and production: Educational Heretics Press

Cover design: John Haxby

Printed by Esparto, Slack Lane, Derby DE22 3DS

Contents

When Learning Becomes Your Enemy:
the relationship between education, spiritual dissent and economics

Introduction

My aim in this study is to map, first historically and then in the contemporary situation, the relationship between education, politics and economics in the west and, more specifically, in the United Kingdom. The use of the term spiritual dissent in the title may seem strange to many readers. My intention in using this term is to draw attention to something I find lacking in our mentality today. It is not meant to convey any specifically religious sense of the idea of 'spirituality'. Rather, I use it in relation to the idea of the political will of the libertarian (or dissenting) tradition which sought to bring about change based on direct political and social action. Sometimes there was a religious conviction that motivated them and, at other times not. In both cases I discern a sense of 'spiritual' conviction connected to a sense of social justice. I use the term 'spiritual' partly to restore this sense of political will and dissenting spirit to our understanding of it.

This book is the outcome of shifts in my own perception. As a teacher and a parent, the former for over thirty years and the latter for twenty three, just five years ago I reached a point where my understanding of my place and role in society and my profession became seriously confused. On the margins I have suffered confusion for many years, since being a teenager certainly but this was new, an all-enveloping confusion as to what was going on. My values no longer fitted within the context of the society in which I now found myself to be living but I could not work out exactly what had gone wrong. That is when the research that presents itself in this book began.

I remember at university, as the nineteen-sixties turned into the seventies, a particular thought crossing my mind. Its significance is clear from the fact that it has stayed in my memory ever since, but I only started to recall it again in recent years as an antidote to what was happening around me: 'I can think what I like'. This mantra, like all mantras, acts as a means of empowerment either for or against the pervading forces in the world.

At the time it was the gift of an education system fostering liberalism, even libertarianism, now it is an anacronistic relic of that time. The expected response to such a statement now (with the anarchistic suggestion it conveys) is 'But you can't do what you like'. This conveys the problem: the prevalent fear today of people thinking independently in case the actions that ensue do not obey the script for 'the common good'. This book investigates why that fear exists, what the appeal to a common good entails, and what it conceals in relation to education. This is the reason it is entitled *When Learning Becomes Your Enemy*, with due acknowledgement to Paolo Friere.

Being both a teacher and a parent involves interesting dilemmas. Our three children all reacted differently to the values that predominated in the home environment. These have been expressed both directly and indirectly, in the ethos and topics of conversation that have prevailed. The children, as they grew older, were assimilated into the further experiences of socialisation: within schooling and its ethos, within formal learning in the curriculum, through friendship groups and antagonism from other groups, and with the influence of individual teachers.

There is, importantly, the pressure of expectations derived from the home environment. Most often, parents receive an understanding of the effect of these from their own children first, not from their own recognitions or conscious observations. For example, in relation to our three children, the first, Kate, had a determination to do well and please us.

She had the academic ability and disposition to pursue this successfully in terms of her achievements (I come back to the question of achievement in chapter four).

The second, Sam, was more interested in his friendship group than his studies. He achieved enough to go on to higher education but had no particular interest in education, as it was presented to him in school or sixth form, for its own sake. He has always opposed the pressure to do well and study conscientiously for exams as a measure of achievement.

The third, Polly, is ambitious in terms of her education relating to a chosen profession. For her, education has a professional utility. You do it because of 'what you want to become'. The profession has changed over the years but the principle of utility has not.

So, three children, all from the same family, who reacted to schooling in different ways: eagerness to learn for its own sake, disaffection at the constraints imposed, seeing it as a means to an end. All three have been critical of some teachers and praised others. All three have been critical of their parents. They all have different attitudes toward their education. They have been fortunate in terms of ability and home support.

I would contend that the supportive environment of their home life has contributed as much toward educational development as their schooling. They might disagree with me. One of the features of their home life has been discussion on innumerable topics - which for me has been a joy. Another feature has been been parental pressure and expectation. J. D. Salinger famously remarked that parents should treat their children as guests in their own house. This has informed my understanding of bringing up my own children. But there is more. At a certain point the house is theirs not just yours, because a sense of belonging and territory demands that and these are intimately related to ownership in more than a literal sense: ownership of thoughts and convictions. Again, this is a privilege, but it ought to be a right. These notions of privilege and rights, related to power and control are at the heart of the argument I pursue and are considerations that have resulted in the writing of it in relation to changes in my perception.

The opinion I now hold, regarding the shaping and restructuring of institutionalised education in this country and beyond I have summarised below. The chapters in this book seek to investigate how we arrived at the situation we now have, what the significant influences are on this situation, and how we might respond to it.

Education is based on the values a society or community is committed to. In the West these values are purported to be democratic. Government pronouncements on family values, parenting, education, citizenship and many other matters seek to convince us that democratic ideals shape the changes that are taking place in these areas and that our society will become more democratic as a result.

I shall argue that this is a subterfuge which seeks to convince us that democratic values and free market capitalism must proceed hand in hand in order that we have a society which offers both opportunity and prosperity, on the one hand, and fairness and justice, on the other. My argument is that the balancing of these values has been, and is increasingly, awry. Rather, free market capitalism is the dominant force to which the notion of democratic values must adhere. The result is a cosmetic veneer of democratic rhetoric used to justify economically anti-democratic practices.

This decorative edifice expressing a concern for morality and values, which is so prominent today, seeks to cloak injustice by weaving the spell of progress, prosperity and lifestyle. The point being made is that progress and prosperity (the economics) are passed off as the necessary basis for a safe, civilised and just society and a pleasurable individual lifestyle. Once this is believed, it becomes implausible to question the economic basis of our society, since by doing so you are perceived to be seeking to subvert the pursuit of justice, happiness, individual freedom, etc.

The argument is spelt out as follows. We need to compete in a global economy, therefore our children need to be educated in order to have the skills to do so. For this to be effective we must assess their development, in terms of competencies, and measure the standard they achieve at any given age. They must take advantage of the opportunity of education (schooling) then they will be successful (gain a place at university) and, subsequently, have a well-paid career. This then provides the basis of a stable family life and, in turn, good educational and career opportunities for their children. The logic of the argument is seamless. Why should it be challenged? One reason might be that the basis of it is competition (the creation of winners and losers). Another might be that its basis is solely economic (wealth creation). For every economically stable family you create another (perhaps many more) unstable ones, whether in this country or elsewhere in the world. For every academically successful child you create one (or more than one) who is unsuccessful, or at least less successful and less able to compete in relation to employment opportunities (whether in this country or globally).

These negative effects are not advertised. This attempt at stratification (league tables for schools and the setting of children in schools are two strategies employed), and the narrow nationalistic aims of such an argument, would be two reasons for questioning it. But those who do so are abused as 'conservatives' or 'wreckers' by the present Prime Minister, Tony Blair.

The vision is that all will benefit from the progress that will ensue from this economic strategy, and that this progress is evidenced by an ever greater capacity to satisfy our wants (for example, in relation to consumer goods to which I turn below). To challenge this vision is to be subversive. To suggest we encourage children to challenge it must therefore be something not far removed from child abuse, and certainly not to their advantage. Nevertheless, my argument is that this is precisely what we need to do and to do so, turning to the subject of the first chapter in this study, we can start by asking the question 'How did we get here?'

Chapter one

How did we get here?

"Who controls the present controls the past,
Who controls the past controls the future."
(Orwell 1949)

"Take the reverse of the current custom and you will nearly
always do right."
(Rousseau 1993: 60)

Here I offer two parallel accounts. The first focuses on the rise of capitalism in the historical period proceeding from the industrial revolution. The second charts a largely forgotten history of dissent proceeding from the period of the English Civil War.

The industrial age

The industrial age which allowed the situation we are now witnessing to evolve, as Walter Benjamin observed, was given its *"cue in the advent of machines"* out of which emerged *"the amorality of the business world and the false morality enlisted in its service"*. (Benjamin 1999: 5). In his commentary on this, Benjamin refers to Fourier and his utopian idea of a socialist community made possible by the emergence of the mechanistic age, in which *"this mechanism made of men produces the land of milk and honey"* (ibid: 5). It was in the Paris Arcades, observes Benjamin, that Fourier conceived his vision *"...whereas they originally serve commercial ends, they become, for him, places of habitation"* (ibid: 5). Places which *"restore human beings to relationships in which morality becomes superfluous"* (ibid: 5). Fourier's vision that overcoming conditions of scarcity through production would bring about a society in which not only materially want would be erased but, as a result, so would the dysfunctions and inequalities of human relationships, now appears naïve in the extreme. It suggests a blindness to the inherent greed that afflicts us. But Fourier's naivete is surpassed by our own, over 170 years later (Fourier wrote *Nouveau Tableaux de Paris* in 1828). Our naivete consists in thinking that, despite the history of exploitation that has riven the period of history from the industrial revolution to the present, we are in the midst of increasing progress toward an ever better future. Such is the pervasive force of the message with which we are presented.

Prophets of the past, like Benjamin, contrarily judged that the World Exhibitions of the mid-nineteenth century, proffering the same allure as the Arcades in their display of merchandise and achievement, were *"places of pilgrimage to the commodity fetish"* (Benjamin 1999:7). They identified the march of the future more correctly. In fact, Benjamin's observation on commodity fetishism is precisely what we witness at a more sophisticated level in the metamorphosis from commodity manufacturing into branding. Perversely, branding allows commodity fetishism to act as a replacement for spiritual fulfilment and a license for amorality at the same time. It is able to do so because of our willingness to believe in the economic prophecy of free market capitalism, and its false promises, that underpin corporate practices. Following Benjamin, both Guy Debord and Jean Baudrillard later take up this theme with the identification of the spectacle that commodity fetishism has turned into. *"The life of the consumer becomes increasingly absurd...able to find identity only in the act of pointless consumption"*, (Plant 1992: 25; see Debord 1977), as *"the circulation of commodities almost becomes an end in itself, quite regardless of the subjects who buy, sell and produce them."* (Plant 1992: 35; see Debord 1977 and Baudrillard 1968).

Just as Fourier underestimated the capacity of capitalism to harness industrial innovation to its own ends, so too, in our age of technological and digital advance, it is possible to believe that innovation will necessarily herald the introduction of a more democratic society. Kevin Kelly, a countercultural activist and writer, made the assumption in the 1990s that *networks*, created through on-line communication and the internet, would connect everything to everything else, making possible the distribution of knowledge and power uncontrollable by governments. The complex organism of the network would enable 'utilizing the timeless, anti-hierarchical principles of distributed intelligence' through the facility of the free market (Frank 2001: 57-8). What is interesting in both Fourier's and Kelly's views is the presumption that new technology will transform society by virtue of the possibilities that the technology itself offers. There is no consideration of how that technology might be harnessed by those who seek power in order to dominate rather than liberate. Such naivete can also be found in the writings of Adam Smith:

> *"Servants, labourers and workmen...make up the far greater part of every great political society. But what improves the circumstances of the greater part can never be regarded as an inconveniency to the whole. No society can surely be flourishing and happy, of which the far greater part of the members are poor and miserable. It is but equity, besides, that they should feed, clothe and lodge the whole body of the people, should have such a share of the produce of their own labour as to be tolerably well fed, clothed and lodged."*
> (Smith 1937: 78-9)

The ethical expectations expressed above derive from Smith's earlier work on moral sentiments. In support of his view of the benign landlord and the rich he resorts to the 'invisible hand' of 'Providence':

> *"They (the rich) are led by an invisible hand to make nearly the same distribution of the necessities of life,*

which would have been made, had the earth been divided into equal portions among all its inhabitants...When Providence divided the earth among a few lordly masters, it neither forgot nor abandoned those who seemed to have been left out in the partition. These last too enjoy their share of all it produces."
(Smith 1976: 184)

And, in support of such a view, there were merchants who shared its utopian spirit:

"Methinks I wou'd not have you not only learn the Method of Merchantize...merely as a means of getting Wealth: it will be well worth your pains to study it as a Science, to see how it is founded in Reason, and the Nature of Things; how it promotes Humanity...by mutual Benefits diffusing mutual Love from Pole to Pole."   (Lillo 1731)

Thus, the 'trickle down' theory, so important to statements made by Tony Blair and other western leaders today was, for Smith, understood as dependent upon a moral sentiment, dependent, in turn, on the invisible workings of Providence. It was not an economic law of capitalism and unrestricted free trade. It was a sentiment of the times born of a certain worldview to which Smith subscribed. That sentiment no longer holds sway, as it did for Smith, thus the distribution of such wealth can no longer be expected. Indeed, writing later in 1844 it was Marx who exposed its lack of effect on entrepreneurial practice:

"...the alienation of the worker is expressed thus: the more he produces, the less he can consume; the more value he creates, the less value he has...labour produces fabulous things for the rich, but misery for the poor. Machines replace labour, and jobs diminish, while other workers turn into machines..."
(Marx 1977: 69-70)

And it was Engels who spelt this out in illustrative detail in *The Condition of the Working Class in England* (Engels 1987).

The significance of observing this shift in expectation and practice is that it alerts us to the following:

- the importance of spiritual and moral sentiment and conviction in determining the use of capital;
- that capitalism, as an economic system is, as a theory, amoral and, in practice, immoral;
- that moral sentiment can be preserved as a rhetorical device, adapted to the spirit of the age, in order to cloak and protect unjust entrepreneurial practice, rather than underpin economic activity;
- that we cannot presume that an economic system, of itself, will result in any prescribed outcomes in relation to humanitarian concern (for example, the prevalent notion that since prosperity will inevitably and eventually lead to prosperity for all we must pursue wealth creation as efficiently as possible).

Given this analysis we might expect that, for the majority of the world's population, a deregulated free market economy will lead to a Hobbesian existence, reflecting the world of nature, being red in tooth and claw. This, of itself, would be nothing new, given that, according to recent statistics, if you have food in the refrigerator, clothes on your back, a roof overhead and a place to sleep...you are richer than 75% of this world. We might, however, expect such a situation to deteriorate rather than improve if the idea of the free market and the de-regulation of economic practice persists. Thus, we come to the question of how domination comes about, and is maintained, in relation to technological innovation.

The libertarian tradition

Writing in 1985, as a preface to Joyce Marlow's book on the Tolpuddle Martyrs, Neil Kinnock, the former leader of the Labour Party, remarks:

"In Britain the Government has used its power to promote perceptible change away from a confident consensus about the freedom of institutions and individuals...The conditions of the 1830s are too deeply buried to return. But when obedience is demanded in place of loyalty, and deference in place of respect, then authoritarian attitudes are being resurrected from the past. That is why it is well for rulers to remember not just the Martyrs of Tolpuddle but also the lessons that their experience taught."
(Marlow 1985: 9-10)

Kinnock's remarks are noteworthy, first because he identifies the resurrection of authoritarianism, still prevalent in the present Labour government, and because, implicitly, he suggests that we can no longer connect with the conditions of the 1830s since they are too buried to return. My attempt here is to conduct an exhumation. Unless we recognise the burial of the tradition of dissent we cannot recognise the legacy upon which any resistance to the present authoritarianism can be based. It is important to note that the Tolpuddle Martyrs were largely self-educated men. Marlow records the first one to be arrested, George Loveless. When he was accosted by the local constable, James Brine, the following conversation ensued:

"Brine: I have a warrant for you, from the magistrates.
Loveless: What is its contents, sir?
Brine: Take it for yourself, you can read it as well as I can.
Loveless, who could almost certainly read far better than the constable, took the document. The charge was of having participated in an illegal oath, remarks Marlow." (ibid: 13)

This exchange would be comical if the results were not so tragic. Loveless was a Methodist, who at that time, were objects of persecution on the basis of being seditious. Despite the labour as an agricultural worker that Loveless carried out he was unable to support his family and, taking steps to remedy this injustice, which seemed to him reasonable and legal, it led to transportation. Whilst held up as heroes within the labour and trade union movements that followed, the Tolpuddle Martyrs hardly impinge on our consciousness today.

Prior to this we can cite the dissident activity of the major figure Tom Paine. Paine was instrumental to the success of both the American and French Revolutions occurring, from the beginning of the American Revolution to the end of the French, between 1775 and 1815.

Mark Philp writes of Paine that *"he was prosecuted in Britain less for what he said than for the fact that it was not confined to 'the judiscious reader'"*, but was reaching those *"whose minds cannot be supposed to be conversant with subjects of this sort...the ignorant, the credulous, the desperate"* (Philp 1995: xxiii). My own concern has a certain parallel with Paine's in that the disenfranchised that Paine sought to reach still exist: the ignorant, those with a lack of education; the credulous, including those who have been educated; and the desperate, those who are bewildered by a society that does not exist to serve their interests. Children and young people fall into all of these categories. It is arguable that their rights and empowerment are less well served than most others within our social system. Our educational system is often the instrumental means to ensuring this, rather than achieving the opposite effect.

Godwin, a contemporary of Paine, and an aide to him in the publication and distribution of the *Rights of Man*, wrote in *Political Justice* that, *"No creature in human form will be expected to learn anything but because he desires it and has some conception of its utility and value"* (Woodcock 1963: 83). Godwin's vision is utopian but it provides the necessary distinction between an education system presently in place and a radical alternative that is, foremost, a respecter of rights and individuals rather than duties and government.

Deeply ingrained in Paine's social and political thought was a division between society and government; the two were opposed in value and function. It is, possibly, our present inability to make a clear distinction between the two that creates a lack of critical understanding of political and economic trends today. This distinction is at the heart of the dissenting tradition. In *Common Sense* Paine begins:

> *"Some writers have so confounded society with government as to leave little or no distinction between them; whereas they are not only different but have different origins. Society is produced by our wants, and government by our wickedness; the former promotes our happiness* **positively** *by uniting our affections, the latter* **negatively** *by restraining our vices. The one encourages intercourse, the other distinctions. The first is a patron, the last is a punisher."*

> *"Society in every state is a blessing, but government even in its best state is a necessary evil; in its worst state an intolerable one..."*
> (Philp 1995: 5)

Within our present centralised educational system, where the imposition of government directives is such an insistent force, Paine's judgement on government can be illustrated. Within religious education, 'thinkers' on the subject have been marginalised. The reason for this, in one Ofsted inspector's view, is that they cannot agree. Thus, the best course of action is for Ofsted to determine how the subject should be taught and learned. The proposal is that it should deal with issues in much the same way as the history curriculum. For example, as in a question on Oliver Cromwell: *'Was Cromwell a hero or a villain?'*

So, let us imagine answers to this question. Considering Cromwell's contemporaries, from the Leveller and Digger perspective presumably the latter judgement, as from a Royalist perspective, but from a Parliamentarian one presumably the former. We may allow for some qualification of the judgement, from the children's reflections on the question; in some respects the former and in others the latter. But what is going on here? First, the theorists are marginalised because they do not agree. Second, the centralised government agency decide what is to be taught and how. Third, the children are encouraged to debate critically an issue of significant historical importance and, presumably, since there would be no point otherwise, to disagree.

Why are we encouraging the capacity to debate critically amongst children but not amongst academics, educationalists and adults? Why should it be valuable in the classroom but not for government? Why should government wish children to develop this capacity when it is of no apparent value in adult educational circles unless it results in agreement? Perhaps, here we have a situation that Paine could not have envisaged in his time. Education has been extended to those who would previously have been counted amongst the ignorant, but it is controlled by government. Thus, the education Paine sought to espouse through his publications is now controlled and regulated by government itself. And, from Godwin's perspective, what is the point of this, considering Cromwell only has some relevance and utility if he impinges on the learner's desires? But the reason for studying Cromwell is according to the government's desires not the child's.

It is difficult to escape the view that children are not meant to arrive at radical conclusions. The point of studying Cromwell is to view him through the cultural, social and political norms of our present society, as well as appreciating his significance in his own time. We look back on Cromwell as though we have progressed beyond him. This is an unstated presumption of the enquiry, which will be suffused with the values and ethos of present day society. It will be an 'academic' exercise, except in the hands of a dissenting teacher. In *The Rights of Man* Paine argues that:

> "*Great part of that order which reigns among mankind is not the effect of government. It has its origin in the principles of society and the natural constitution of men...The mutual dependence and reciprocal interest which man has upon man...create that great chain of connexion which holds it together...Common interest regulates their concerns and forms of law; and the laws which common usage ordains, have a greater influence than the laws of government".*
> (Woodcock 1963: 48-9)

This is close to what the anarchist Kropotkin meant by mutual aid and what the fellow anarchist and novelist Tolstoy meant by love. The exorcising of government, in our society, appears to represent a loss of the civilising agency that holds society together, but that is precisely what government presents in its own justification. In terms of education this justifies government agencies in their desire to tell schools and parents what their children need to learn to succeed. The French anarchist Proudhon, in the mid-nineteenth century, envisaged education as being controlled by parents and teachers without government. This would be a state of affairs closer to the principles identified above of mutual or common interest.

Returning to the question of why these visions of the future society did not establish themselves, we can note something of the tensions that have created our present condition and compromised the dissenting vision through economic interest. Walker, in 1794, wrote critically of the Dissenters as follows:

> "*Dissenters...have as a body constantly fallen short of their own principles; through fear or some other motive they have been so strongly the advocates of an Overstrained Moderation that they have rather been the*

enemies than the friends of those who have ventured the
most and effected the most for the rights of the people."
(Walker 1794: 125)

E. P. Thompson's commentary on this statement provides
further insight as to why this compromise of principle and
practice should have occurred. He suggests:

> *"We see here, perhaps, a tension between London and*
> *the industrial centres. The Dissenters at Manchester,*
> *the members of the Old Meeting at Birmingham or the*
> *Great Meeting at Leicester, included some of the*
> *largest employers in the district. Their attachment to*
> *civil and religious liberty went hand in hand with their*
> *attachment to the dogmas of free trade...But their*
> *enthusiasm for civil liberty melted away with the*
> *publication of* Rights of Man..."
> (Thompson 1968: 57-8)

This observation is prescient and affords us some
understanding of the way in which the tensions between
dissent directed toward governance, from the libertarian
perspective, and similar dissent, from an entrepreneurial
direction, have resulted in a state of affairs in which the
latter can claim the ambitions of the former to substantiate
their claims in the contemporary market place. The
sophistication, and duplicity, with which this has been
accomplished will be discussed in the next chapter.

Change in the moral order

What started to erode in the final years of the eighteenth
century was an older moral economy to be replaced by that
of the free market that emerged with the industrial
revolution. This economy was based on the idea that the
populous should not be exploited by the inflation of prices of
staple foods, bread was the defining example, due to the
exportation or restriction, (hoarding), of goods entering the
market. 1795 was the final point at which these activities
were legally outlawed by the Lord Chief Justice Kenyon,

who ruled that, *"forestalling and engrossing remained offences at common law"* (Thompson 1968: 72). Beyond this date prosecutions ceased. Food riots were a continuous feature of uprisings in the latter half of the eighteenth century, but the French Revolution brought a backlash. There was fear that the underclasses might revolt in England as they had in France, and the success of the distribution of Tom Paine's *Rights of Man* was evidence of their desire for education and interest in political activity and direct action.

At this time, states Thompson, *"The law was hated, but it was also despised"*, and *"Such "riots" were popularly regarded as acts of justice, and their leaders held as heroes"* (Thompson 1968: 66,70). In response, the majority of sentences to death in the courts became based on crimes related to the economy. Here was a notable change in the moral idea of what constituted the most serious criminal activity - it now embraced economic dissent - the communitarian character of the older moral economy was legally displaced. Such a change in moral consciousness both legitimises the de-regulated market, enabling the pursuit of profit as an end in itself, and de-legitimises dissent expressed on the basis that the result is the creation of poverty and marginalisation. Institutionally, the judgement of the courts precedes and directly influences judgements as to what constitutes education, schooling and learning.

The framing of our education system

When we consider the way our education system has been framed in the light of the issues discussed above we may cite the following influences. The education system in this country was defined by the industrial revolution. Prior to this historical period the underclass, poor or unpropertied had no need of education other than being consigned to the duties that the propertied classes required. In my own family, on my mother's side, work within the Earl of Derby's estate or in his household constituted their lot. With the industrial revolution, however, there was a greater need to produce a skilled workforce that satisfied a national industrial economy based on trade. The State, as Adam Smith remarked below, was better served by instructing the inferior classes than not.

"A man without the proper use of the intellectual faculties of a man is, if possible, more contemptible than even a coward, and seems to be mutilated and deformed in a still more essential part of the character of human nature. Though the State was to derive no advantage from the instruction of the inferior ranks of people, it would still deserve its attention that they should not be altogether uninstructed. The State, however, derives a considerable advantage from their instruction. The more they are instructed, the less liable they are to the delusions of enthusiasm and superstition, which among ignorant nations frequently occasion the most dreadful disorders. An instructed and intelligent people, besides, are always more decent and orderly than a stupid one...and more likely to obtain the respect of their lawful superiors."

(Barnard 1961: 45-6)

By contrast Paine's observations on the benefits of educating the nation are somewhat different in purpose.

"...a nation under a well regulated government should permit none to remain uninstructed...By adopting this method...ignorance will be banished from the rising generation, and the number of the poor will hereafter become less, because their abilities by the aid of education will be greater."

(Barnard: 46-7)

Placed in the context of the times, it is salutary to note the significance of the differences between Smith and Paine. Smith was arguing against a body of opinion that regarded the education of the poor as unnecessary and positively dangerous. Thus, his argument seeks to oppose the opinion that education would produce unrest. Writing before the effects of the French Revolution, Smith was attempting to balance the need for skilled workers against the fear of a subjugated but educated class. In contrast, Paine was attempting to spread insurrection, and thus appealing to the possibilities inherent in raising the poor to a higher state through education. The arguments presented in the two texts are politically incommensurable.

The establishment position, including that of the established church, was decidedly against the education of the masses. When Samuel Whitbread put forward his *Parochial Schools Bill* in 1807 the response of the Archbishop of Canterbury was that

> "...it would go to subvert the first principles of education in this country, which had hitherto been, and he trusted would continue to be, under the control and auspices of the establishment."
> (Barnard 1961: 55; Hansard, vol ix, 1178, Aug 11, 1807)

There was even the view that it was not even in the interests of the poor for them to be educated.

> "However specious in theory the project might be of giving education to the labour classes of the poor, it would be prejudicial to their morals and happiness; it would teach them to despise their lot in life, instead of making them good servants in agriculture and other laborious employments. Instead of teaching them subordination, it would render them fractious and refactory, as was evident in the manufacturing counties; it would enable them to read seditious pamphlets...and publications against Christianity."
> (response of Davies Giddy, Barnard 1961: 55; Hansard, vol ix, 798, July 13, 1807)

The above response makes particularly clear the fear of the establishment that what had happened abroad could also happen in England, and the repressive response that sanctifies itself by appealing to the value of ignorance for the ignorant. There was also the Evangelical view that went further in justifying inequality. Not only were the propertied classes rightly superior, but inequality was ordained by God, *"Inequalities of fortune in this world must be accepted without demure because they would be redressed in the next"* (Barnard: 50).

As a result, of course, the poor really had nothing to grumble about. But what we really learn from investigating these attitudes is that every argument will be used to protect the status quo by those whom the status quo serves, and that every effort will be made to persuade those whom it does not serve that it is really in their interests. Exposing this outrageous and cynical duplicity is the only means of creating awareness of the corruption that lies at the heart of our education system. This corruption is sustained by those who serve within education as Edmund Holmes, the disillusioned first Chief Inspector of Schools, observed in 1911.

> *"...the way in which the teacher too often conducts his school leads one to infer that the intuitive, instinctive side of him – the side that is nearest to practice – has somehow or other held intercourse with the inner meaning of that 'truism' (the necessity of child-centredness) which he repeats so glibly, and has rejected it as antagonistic to the traditional assumptions on which he bases his life. Or perhaps this work of subconscious criticism and rejection has been and is being done for him, either by the spirit of the age or by the genius of the land in which he lives."*
> (Shute 1998: 7)

Paulo Freire's determination was to expose how education either worked for or against those being educated and that, in practice, institutionalised education did the latter, not the former. As Shaull observes:

> *"There is no such thing as a neutral educational process. Education either functions as an instrument which is used to facilitate the integration of the younger*

> *generation into the logic of the present system and bring about conformity to it, or it becomes 'the practice of freedom', the means by which men and women deal critically and creatively with reality and discover how to participate in the transformation of their world. The development of an educational methodology that facilitates this process will inevitably lead to tension and conflict in our society."*
>
> (Freire 1972: 14)

A further observation made by Shaull, however, cannot be said to apply to the consciousness of most young people today:

> *"The young perceive that their right to say their own word is stolen from them, and that few things are more important than the struggle to win it back. And they also realise that the educational system today – from kindergarten to university – is their enemy."*
>
> (ibid: 13)

How is it that our present educational system, although criticised in terms of its management, is not criticised in terms of its values and its rhetorical deceitfulness? What has happened to the dissenting tradition, from the Levellers and Diggers of the Civil War period, through Tom Paine, to Paolo Frere? How is it that we are blind to 'meconnaissance' – *"the process whereby power relations are perceived not for what they objectively are, but in a form which renders them legitimate in the eyes of the beholder"*? (Bottomore T. in Bourdieu and Passeron 1990: xxii). Bourdieu and Passeron's proposition, to which we shall return again later, that *"All pedagogic action is, objectively, symbolic violence"* (ibid: 5), itself reads strangely to those who have accepted a state of affairs: capitalistic values and conformism, to which there appears no contrary. This alerts us to one thing that modern education does well: blind us to our own self-interest by providing us with what it tells us is in our own self-interest. And 'self-interest', within a capitalist frame of reference, is the dominant dogma. Thus, educational repression is presented as a 'rhetoric of opportunity'. There is no objectivity to hold onto here. It is a question of whose values are legitimated, and it is with this question in mind that my enquiry into education and its relationship with contemporary society begins.

References Chapter 1

Barnard, H. (1961) *A History of English Education From 1760*, London: University of London Press.

Baudrillard, Jean (1968) *Le Systeme des Objets*, Paris: Denoel-Gonthier.

Benjamin, W. (1999) *The Arcades Project*, Cambridge, Mass. and London, England: The Belknap Press of Harvard University Press.

Bourdieu, Pierre and Passeron, Jean-Claude (1990) *Reproduction in Education, Society and Culture*, 2nd edition, London: Sage.

Debord, Guy (1977) *The Society of the Spectacle*, Detroit: Black and Red.

Engels, F. (1987) *The Conditions of the Working Class in England*, London: Penguin.

Fourier, Charles (1928) *Nouveau Tableaux de Paris: Vol. 1*, Paris: publisher unknown.

Frank, T. (2001) *One Market Under God*, London: Secker and Warburg.

Freire, P. (1972) *Pedagogy of the Oppressed*, Harmondsworth: Penguin.

Lillo, (1731) *The History of George Barnwell, or, the London Merchant*

Marlow, Joyce (1985) *The Tolpuddle Martyrs,* London: Grafton Books.

Marx, Karl (1977) *Economic and Philosophic Manuscripts of 1844,* Moscow: Progress Publishers.

Orwell, George (1949) *Nineteen Eighty-four*, London: Secker and Warburg.

Philp, M. ed. (1995) *Thomas Paine: Rights of Man, Common Sense and Other Political Writings*, Oxford: Oxford University Press.

Plant, Sadie (1992) *The Most Radical Gesture: The Situationist International in a Postmodern Age*, London and New York: Routledge.

Rousseau, Jacques (1993) *Emile*, London: Everyman.

Shute, C. (1998) *Edmond Holmes and The Tragedy of Education*, Nottingham: Educational Heretics Press.

Smith, Adam (1937) *The Wealth of Nations,* New York: Random House.

Smith, Adam (1976) *The Theory of Moral Sentiments*, Oxford: Clarendon Press.

Thompson, E. P. (1968) *The Making of the Working Class*, Harmondsworth: Penguin.

Walker, T. (1974) *Review of Some Political Events in Manchester,*

Woodcock, G. (1963) *Anarchism*, Harmondsworth: Penguin.

Chapter two

The present state of affairs

The branding of education

The right to domination is never advertised as such in democratic societies, rather domination is gained by appeal to its very opposite: liberty. This play on paradox is at the heart of strategies employed by those who have gained influence over today's global economy. In attempts to immunise themselves from charges of injustice their claim is that they are just responding to the demand expressed through the will of the people. Thus, those who seek domination are precisely those who suppress that will through regulation: governments, trade unions and liberal intellectuals. These are the elite figures and bodies used to exercising power and influence: the suppressers of the popular will (Frank 2001: 45-7).

As Frank records in dwelling on the statements made by Jeffrey Bell, a former aide to Ronald Reagan, in the latter's publication *Populism and Elitism* (1992: 3):

"Elitism '...was a term correctly applied to those who believe in 'the decision-making ability of one or more elites, acting on behalf of other people' [thus]...Ronald Reagan, whose deregulatory and tax-reducing fervor could be portrayed as faith in the public's ability to manage their own money, came out populist; while Michael Dukakis, along with anyone else who believed in regulation, was an elitist."

(Frank 2001: 45)

As Frank mentions, this was a *"clever inversion device"* (ibid: 45) since it inverted the term's meaning as used in the Populist movement of the 1890s in the United States and removed the significant issue of relative wealth, which was central to the Populist cause. This new 'populism' acted as an energising focus for corporate and multi-national companies as it constructed a climate of moral injustice within which business Goliaths could be seen to be acting benevolently for the common person rather than, as had been incorrectly perceived previously, out of self interest. Thus, a double injustice had to be rectified and the previous delusions as to the character and purposes of capital dispelled.

Frank's analysis as to how this was implemented depended upon the upturn in the financial market in 1999, when the Dow Jones Industrial Average crossed the 10,000 mark. Such a bull market leads to the investment fairy tales so common now in any subway advertisement. The idea was that any ordinary person could invest in the market and receive a share of its riches as a result. This way you could fulfil your dreams and prove the populist power of deregulated democracy at the same time. The two were not incompatible, after all. It was the *"inalienable right"* of *"every man and woman...to make money - and lots of it"* declared *Individual Investor* magazine, in copies of an 'Investment Manifesto' handed out around Manhattan (Frank 2001: 90). Thus, entrepreneurs and financiers were depicted in various manifestations of spin as the inaugurators of a populist revolution that bore the values of Woody Guthrie: this land becomes your land through your investments (see Frank 2001: 91).

Frank's analysis is complemented by those of others, notably Klein (2000), and Monbiot (2000). Inside the front cover of Klein's book is recorded the observation of Indonesian writer Y.B. Mangunwijaya on July 16, 1998: *"You might not*

*see things yet on the surface, but underground, it's already
on fire"* (Klein 2000).

The fire metaphor, as it can be applied to the present state of
global affairs, does not relate to the flames of revolution
against corporate practices but, contrarily, to the stoking up
of bonfires of human suffering, located and fuelled by the
corporate will. On the surface we do not see them. What we
see is what we desire to see: the commodities that serve our
lust for a distinctive and admired sense of individual
identity. How does this strange state of affairs arise? Klein
begins to chart it when she observes and reports on the
'underground', by visiting the Asian sweatshops herself. In
one report, from Jakarta, she remarks:

> *"By now these Indonesian workers were used to people
> like me: foreigners who come to talk to them about the
> abysmal conditions in the factories where they cut, sew
> and glue for multinational companies like Nike, the Gap
> and Liz Claiborne...Here they were all young, some of
> them as young as fifteen...(earning) the equivalent of
> US$2 per day...being forced to work long hours of
> overtime but (not) being paid at the legal rate for their
> trouble...In this part of the world, hundreds of workers
> every year burn to death because their dormitories are
> located upstairs from firetrap sweatshops."*
> (Klein 2000: xv-xvi)

The late 20th century outcome of what Benjamin observed
concerning the Paris Arcades and the commodity fetish is
recorded by both Klein and Monbiot. But the shift from
marketing manufactured hardware to marketing spiritual
software based on identity and image was the crucial one:
branding. Branding operates at the microcosmic level of the
individual and the macrocosmic level of global identity.
IBM's campaign entitled *Solutions for a Small Planet* is an
example of the latter, with its therapeutic message of
technology bringing about a harmonious and humanitarian
global society providing the façade to hide its increasing

control and extortionate profits, (and suggesting that such profits are justified in the light of its potential to succeed in its utopian vision). Such a campaign is a barely concealed manifesto for control, feeding off the democratic sensibilities of liberalism; again part of the decorative values rhetoric.

An example of the former is Nike's *Just do it!* campaign. Incongruously, I came across this brand slogan on the backboard of a basketball net in a fishing village in southern Spain. By its very situatedness in a poor working class area dependent for its community survival on its fishing catch, the slogan verified the social concern of the corporation in extending its message to the young of such a community. Along the rest of the coast, on either side, were the continuous apartment developments offering second homes for the comparatively wealthy. In all of these developments the Nike brand was equally conspicuous, and not at all incongruous. I think what we can observe here is not the egalitarian vision of the sportswear company, but its desire to introduce a certain type of individualistic ambition to the young of a community that can be interpreted, within that location, as 'you can aspire to the social status of those in neighbouring middle class apartments. It is your choice'. The fact that the slogan was on a basketball backboard, in this case, references to the icon Michael Jordan both as inspiration and example.

All interpretation of this sort is conjectural in character, on the surface. It is only when you investigate the values of the company in relation to its business practices that more benign interpretations become impossible to sustain. That does not rule out the inherent duplicity involved as a tactic in these branding games, of course. And, most significantly, the slogans themselves are imbued with a particular values message that the company wishes to convey which, at one and the same time, both promotes its own sense of concern for individuals and community *and* extends the influence of capitalism's values orientation: individualism, choice and competition.

Klein refers to this vision of choice as follows, in order to evidence the corporate restriction within which it is envisaged and the community destruction on which it depends:

> *"Everyone has, in one form or another, witnessed the odd double vision of vast consumer choice coupled with Orwellian new restrictions on cultural production and public space. We see it when a small community watches its lively downtown hollow out, as big box discount stores with 70,000 items on their shelves set up on their periphery; exerting their gravitational pull to what James Howard Kunstler describes as 'the geography of nowhere."*
> (Klein 2000: 130)

Monbiot, in greater detail in his case studies, traces the history of such developments in the United Kingdom, notably in Southampton, England (Monbiot 2000: 93-126), and Brecon, Wales (Monbiot 2000: 162-206).

Corporatism, values and education

John Ralston Saul (1997), offers one of the most incisive analyses of the effect of corporatist 'philosophy' on education. He argues for a radical reform of an education system that has increasingly turned toward a utilitarian function. In the process, it has neglected to address the significant values questions related to individual identity and human society. Having been *"co-opted into the corporatist system, becoming obsessed with operating as businesses rather than with instilling deeper philosophical values"* (Britten 1998: 18), it rejects the importance of self-understanding and is uncomfortable with, if not (paradoxically), hostile to non-conformity.

The means of re-orientating education to a free market economy are manifestly bureaucratic:

> *"Management...is the force elected by the New Right to carry through the restructuring of the welfare state. It is the agency which inherits the dismantling of old regimes and provides a new regime, (a new mode of power), around which organisations can be structured."*
>
> (Clarke and Newman 1992: 6, quoted in Gewirtz, Ball, and Bowe 1995: 115-6)

The institutional conflict this new agency generates is one that divides across understandings of democracy embedded in differing foundations: communitarian and free market. The former is identified as outmoded and the latter as open to change and opportunity. This is illustrated in the following summary of the experience in a London comprehensive:

> *"Underlying these events, (conflict in importing this new management model in a London comprehensive), we can see a more fundamental struggle underway...Between an ILEA (Inner London Education Authority) culture and a competitive culture. The first sees the school as serving its local 'community', while the second sees the school in an open and fluid market place. The first, paradoxically perhaps, is seen by senior management...as rooted and entrenched in outmoded ideas. The staff who inhabit this culture are seen as 'captured' by the school's history. The second is seen as dynamic and innovative. It is a culture which is driven by expediency rather than by principle and orientated to financial rather than educational priorities. Interestingly, both camps see themselves as defending comprehensive education. The 'old guard' see comprehensivism as rooted in a particular set of practices and commitments. The new management see the future of comprehensivism...as resting on the achievement of an intake comprised of a cross-section*

of student abilities. Here, then, we see market policies being struggled over within the micro politics of the institution."   (Gewirtz et al. 1995)

The term 'outmoded' used here is, of course, another example of rhetoric rather than argument. It is not to do with 'time' as such, but with 'mode' or fashion, thus old-fashioned is a pejorative requiring no further justification within the new model. It renders the old model manifestly implausible. The purpose of this, as the authors go on to expose, is that, just as we can observe in corporate business practice, the opportunity for choice is the selling point for these operations. But, *"As far as equity is concerned, choice is a dangerous irrelevance".* (ibid: 190)

This new model of democratic education, based on instrumentalist restructuring and lacking any fundamental educational philosophy, has important implications for business. Of this, businessmen themselves have long been well aware. This is evidenced in the following statement that *"A democratic system of education...is one of the surest ways of creating and greatly extending markets for goods of all kinds and especially those goods in which fashion may play a part".*   (Rorty 1934; quoted in Klein 2000: 87)

The new model of democratic education, however, only fulfils its potential once closer partnership with business ensues. Witnessing the shortfalls in government funding set against schools' growing needs, especially in relation to ICT resources, required by curriculum changes introduced by government education agencies operating with the 'new model' may appear to throw education into crisis. But, what has not yet been taken account of is the role businesses can play. This role is unlikely to be that of the neutral benefactor. Examples available pertaining to the United States illustrate how corporations can, by the back door, attempt vital changes affecting the values of schools and higher education. They use such institutions to affirm their own business practices and their value to a democratic society. For example, by contracts ensuing from sponsorship deals, as the following reports reveal:

> *"At South Fork High School in Florida, (where Pepsi has introduced 'Pepsi achievement Awards'), there is a blunt hard-sell arrangement: the school has a clause in its Pepsi contract committing the school to 'make its best effort to maximize all sales opportunities for Pepsi-Cola products."*
>
> (Klein 2000: 91).

At university level a similar form of agreement can also operate:

> *"The University of Kentucky's deal with Nike...has a clause that the company has the right to terminate the five year £25 million contract if the 'University disparages the Nike brand...or takes any other action inconsistent with the endorsement of Nike products."*
>
> (ibid: 97)

The impact of such agreements on everyday decision making, regarding what can and cannot be allowed, is signalled in the following two examples. In a school in Evans, Georgia, which had decided to have a Coca-Cola Day, and invite representatives of that company, one student came wearing a Pepsi-Cola T-shirt, when they all had to wear Coca-Cola T-shirts. He was suspended (Klein:95). More worryingly still, Kent State University Amnesty International Chapter wanted to bring a Free Nigeria Movement speaker to the campus. In April 1998 they applied to the student council for funding. Coca-Cola had exclusive vending rights on the campus. They were asked if he would be speaking negatively about Coca-Cola *"because Coca-Cola does a lot of positive things on our campus like helping organisations and sports"*. They said he would, in relation to the company's involvement in Nigeria. Funding was denied (ibid: 97).

In summary, these corporatist interventions into the education system desire nothing less than to change the policies and values operating within educational institutions to serve their own advantage. The 'new model' of democratic education is an attempt to ensure that such economic opportunities as the above can be made available to these institutions. In order for that to happen the old values must be swept away by new management initiatives. A more philosophical interrogation of how this collusion is affecting the humanities curriculum in higher education is made below in the next section of this paper.

To remain, however, with Coke for a brief space, in order that my argument is not perceived to rely just on isolated examples, I wish to record the research of a 'neutral' observer. The drink was described by one of its executives, William Allen White, as *"the sublimated essence of all that America stands for"* (Pendergrast 1994: 354). We can understand the political implications of such a comment and the effect of the company's aggressive marketing of American free-market values in the following accounts. They are taken from a tableaux of events at the time of the collapse of the Soviet regime and the opening of new markets between 1990 and 1992.

- After the 1989 massacre in Tiananmen Square, Coke continues to sell its drink wherever thirsty Chinese - repressed or repressor - congregate.
- All of Latin America opens to Coke with falling trade barriers and government deregulation to permit higher prices and larger package sizes...In Guatemala, there is relative peace at the actual bottling plant, though several Coca-Cola union workers involved in political theatre are threatened, beaten and murdered.
- Coke moves aggressively into East Germany... transforming ex-Communists into devout Coca-Cola men and women...Sales soar from zero to 1.7 billion drinks in two years.   (Pendergrast: 411-413)

What is so astonishing about this reportage is that Pendergrast remarks at the beginning of his study, *"I've enjoyed taking a more objective view of the Company and its entertaining role in world history. I hope you will, too"* (ibid: xvii). We are presented with the notion of objectivity as a value-free commentary on significant values and political issues engaged in by a soft drinks company that can, more accurately, be understood as an exporter of imperialist American free market values and a restricter of human rights. This serves to illustrate the way in which the denigrating epithet of 'amoral' can be rhetorically transformed into the acceptable liberal catechism as 'objective'. It is precisely the collusion of the liberal educational tradition and liberal values with this stance to which I now turn.

De-centering education

Spanos' *The End of Education* sets out to decenter the approach to higher education. By this he means to expose and remove centralised control. He relates that, following the Vietnam War and the publication of the Harvard Core Curriculum Report in 1978, the aim in higher education in the universities of the United States was to ensure the restoration of the humanities curriculum. This was to be done by basing it upon the world's great literature and protecting it from the 'self-destructive' course it had followed in the 1960s with the disruptive introduction of theoretical analysis in literary studies (Spanos 1993: 1-2). This reclamation of legacy, as it was called, *"the great task of transmitting a culture to its rightful heirs,"* by those who responsibly care, amounted to the *"reclamation of 'our' cultural heritage"* (ibid: 2). These are the phrases of the Report itself. The connection with the Vietnam War was made, using the metaphors of health: *"the recuperation of the good health the nation apparently lost during the turbulent decade of the Vietnam War"* (1993: 1) and the *"healing of the wound"* (1993: 3) caused by civil rights, feminist and student protest movements.

Spanos identifies in this project the attempt to recuperate a national consensus by appeal to a generalized 'we', which includes not only academics themselves but the readers of the *Wall Street Journal* (1993: 3), amongst others who could be counted upon to support it. It is the construction of this naturalized 'we' that he sets out to pursue and, in doing so, advance an alternative account based *"especially...(on) what it leaves unsaid"* (1993: 3). He argues that the construction of a unified cultural heritage to which 'we' all belong is a clever way of excluding difference by way of consensus. What we can all agree on is our cultural heritage. What is disagreed upon is not, as a result, part of that heritage, and can be left out.

This pushes difference to the margins. The centre is presented as the model for progress and civilisation by virtue of it *being* the centre (occupied by the agreed will). By default, those who disagree are marginalised, and thus ignored. This is how dissent is managed, by a process of regulation, apparently democratic because it is based on consensus, which creates the centralisation of power and appears to act for the common good, the 'we'. In doing so it constructs a particular notion of agreed heritage and uniform national identity which can be taught as true and normal. In English education in schools the same process was employed by the Qualifications and Curriculum Authority in the latter half of the 1990s in relation to spiritual and moral education (see Erricker 1998), and into the early twenty first century, this persists in its construction of Citizenship education. Such a process can be well characterised by what Michel Foucault has called 'the disciplinary society' (Foucault 1991).

The display of difference now takes place in a safely domesticated and regulated space. An example of this takes us back to the effect of Branding. Tommy Hilfiger sweatshirts, originally worn by blacks articulating dissent and difference, become 'cool' for white teenagers who want to identify with the style of the original wearers. Identifying with the style does not amount to being imbued with the values of the original. Thus, the display of difference, is happily accommodated within the practices of capitalism. It is the superficial accommodation of the majority to a branding operation that allows them the replacement for a more rooted spiritual and values identity.

Frank records one chief executive of a company recognising that, in the Spanish Civil War soldiers would die with Stalin's names on their lips but one cannot imagine them having the same devotion to a brand name! Equally, when we turn to education, the replacement for education is easily sold in the context of a lack of *critical* investment in the questions of identity and values. It consists in reducing democracy to the agreement that children should learn right from wrong, which consists of no more than learning how to be morally obedient, and gaining the skills that will result in employment. The reward consists in being able to buy what you are told to desire, without troubling the conscience with the human cost involved. That, in sum, is what it means to be a good citizen. It is a long way from Henry Giroux's invocation that:

> *"Education must be understood as producing not only knowledge but also political subjects...[schools must be] places of critical education in the service of creating a public sphere of citizens who are able to exercise power over their own lives and especially over the conditions of knowledge production and acquisition."*
> (Giroux 1996: 688-689)

Indeed, it would seem that schools are the worst place to be if you want education. The ethos of schooling is the inculcation of the importance of not thinking critically about the values of your society, even if you learn to think critically within the values of your society. The latter is regarded as a skill that is marketable; the former is regarded (ironically) as a threat to democracy.

References Chapter 2

Bell, Jeffrey (1992) *Populism and Elitism: Politics in the Age of Equality*, Washington D.C.: Regnery.

Britten, Daniel (1998) 'Free to do as we're told', London: *The Observer Review*, 14 June.

Clarke, J. and Newman, J. (1992) 'Managing to Survive: Dilemas of Changing organisational Forms in the Public Sector', paper presented at Social Policy Association Conference, University of Nottingham, July.

Erricker, C. (1998) 'Spiritual Confusion: a critique of current educational policy in England and Wales', *The International Journal of Children's Spirituality*, 3:1. pp.51-64.

Foucault, M. (1991) *Discipline and Punish: the Birth of the Prison*, London: Penguin.

Frank, T. (2001) *One Market Under God*, London: Secker and Warburg.

Gewirtz, Sharon, Ball, Stephen J., Bowe, Richard (1995) *Markets, Choice and Equity in Education*, Buckingham: Open University Press.

Giroux, Henry A. (1996) 'Towards a Postmodern Pedagogy', in Lawrence Cahoone (ed.) *From Modernism to Postmodernism: An Anthology,* Cambridge, Mass and Oxford: Blackwell. pp. 687-697

Klein, Naomi (2000) *No Logo: taking aim at the brand bullies,* London: HarperCollins.

Monbiot, George (2000) *Captive State: the corporate takeover of Britain*, London: Macmillan.

Pendergrast, Mark (1994) *For God, Country and Coca-Cola*, London: Phoenix.

Rorty, James (1934) *Our Master's Voice*, New York: The John Day Company.

Rousseau, Jean-Jacques (1993) *Emile*, London: The Everyman Library.

Saul John R. (1997) *The Unconscious Civilization*, London: Penguin.

Spanos, William V. (1993) *The End of Education*, Minneapolis and London: University of Minnesota Press.

Chapter three

Political spirituality and the denial of 'education'

Introduction

We ended the last chapter by considering *what* was wrong with education, having reviewed *why* education had gone wrong. In this chapter I wish to outline how we might put it right. Giroux wrote of the importance of politics to democratic education and how that is missing. Below Andrew Samuels, a psychologist, speaks of the effect of this being a lack of a 'political soul'. This chapter assesses why we lack a political will to effect change and how that can be revitalised.

The dissenters crossed religious and non-religious divides, often according to the age in which they lived. The dissenters during the civil war period were located in a largely religious society, those of the nineteenth century were not. This is not the important category to identify. Rather, within any age we must ask why the dissent occurred and what the dissenters had in common. This amounts to an understanding of their political motivations based on the way in which their spiritual convictions, by which I mean their understanding of values and justice, related to the political and social conditions of their times. My argument in this chapter is based on the premise that we have lost the conviction that inspired them and, as a consequence, lost the tradition which they represent. The question is 'How do we restore it?' That is what concerns me here: restoring the will to dissent.

The psychology of collateral damage

Samuels relates that it was John Maynard Keynes, in the 1930s, who made the claim that *"Practical men who believe themselves to be quite exempt from any intellectual influences, are usually the slaves of some defunct economist"* (Samuels 2001: 135). By this I presume he meant that we allow an 'expert' to do our thinking for us. It might also be said that 'spiritual' people who believe themselves to be quite exempt from any political activity are usually the slaves of an irrelevant divinity.

Samuels provides us with a useful starting point. In *Politics on the Couch: Citizenship and the Internal Life* he works towards a transformation of politics from a psychological perspective. This involves addressing the inter-relatedness of spirituality, economics, psychology and politics. In summary, towards the end, he writes:

> *"Our disappointment at liberal democracy's failure to deliver the goods and our growing realization that there are limits to what can be achieved by economic redistribution or altering the constitution strengthen this book's argument: something is missing in contemporary politics that has led to a calamitous denial of the secret life at its core."*
> (Samuels 2001: 205)

At this core is the 'political soul' that yearns for deeper transformations than our political life affords (op-cit). This reference to 'soul' invites the need to address the spiritual and Samuel's identifies a new approach to spirituality being required for the transformation of politics. Spirituality, then, is a *"profoundly democratic commitment to equality"* - a commitment to equality in society rather than equality in the eyes of God - ensuring that the 'non-normal', in psychiatric terms those suffering from syndromes and symptoms, are not *"cast out of the spiritual lifeboat"* (Samuels 2001: 203). Translated into economic terms this is understood as impacting on wealth creation to produce balance rather than wealth equality. It is a rescuing of the idea of the market from capitalism to some degree (Samuels: 2001: 148). It is not a polarised opposition to capitalism but a regulation of the amount of wealth of entrepreneurs by introducing a point at which public or social ownership comes into the frame to prevent the despoilation of human society and the planet on which it depends (op-cit).

In relation to education and the drive toward preparation for increased flexibility of employment, Samuels dwells on the US labour secretary, Robert Reich's, and the then British shadow chancellor, Gordon Brown's, statements in 1994 on training and retraining being the keys to a successful modern economy that entails an education-driven economics. Samuels laments the casual attention paid to the *"huge collective psychological changes being demanded"* and the emotional impact of such a programme (Samuels 2001: 138).

This is humane thinking and rightfully challenges a number of assumptions that pass unquestioned in modern societies in the West, influenced by the impact of free-market economics. The call to pay attention to a more holistic model of individuals and societies; to the spirit and the psyche - the unseen and unmeasurable - in a world caught up in the material and the measurable, is surely appropriate. But my initial concern is why our state of affairs, our social conscience and consciousness, is so perversely stubborn in the lack of attention it is prepared to pay to such matters. Why should this be so and how has such an attitude been legitimated and maintained? At this point, we can make one pertinent observation about the form of words used by the politicians identified above. What is an 'education-driven economics'? Clearly it involves developing the capacity to train and retrain, as stated; therefore it must most obviously identify education as a training programme in 'key' and 'transferable' skills, to be of benefit in the market place. Why is this not called an 'economics-driven education'? For that is what it is. The reversal of words gives us a clue to the way that language is used in the public domain. If education is in the service of economics (economics being stated first), we might be wary of the import of such an idea in a western liberal democracy. If economics is in the service of education (education being stated first), that sounds more healthy and gives us more of a sense of democratic control over, but also toward, wealth production. This sits more easily on our conscience and within our values. But it is a subterfuge that accomplishes three things at the same time. First, a lack of restraint on the pursuit of material wealth; second the transformation of an education system to achieve this; third, the salving of the social conscience. The sum, however, is greater than the parts alone. It also creates a sea change in our consciousness at to what constitutes the norms and values of a western democratic social reality. The change being attended to is an economic one. Other changes arising as a result will be addressed, with more or less attention given to them, with the economic goals in mind.

Zygmunt Bauman takes up similar themes to Samuels but his analyses can progress us still further. In relation to psychological insecurity he speaks in particular of the obscure 'market forces' and inscrutable 'laws of competition' and mysterious 'pressures of globalization' impinging on individuals and communities who are helpless to respond within their specific locations and in relation to their tenure of employment. Negotiation on the basis of their worth or values is simply not an option when confronted with the procedures of 'rationalization' visited upon them by their employers but seeming to be located in some distant and dislocated reality (Bauman 1999: 48-9). The psychological effect of such trauma is disempowerment due to an inability to grasp the specifics of the dislocation involved. There is no-one who represents and can speak to it except in the terms of redundancy and economic sufficiency. Meaningful communication has disappeared into some economic ether or, as Castells describes it, a *"global electronic casino"*, in which, Bauman comments, *"capital and power escape into the hyperspace of pure circulation and are no longer embodied in the 'capitalist' or ruling' classes"* (Bauman 1999: 50). Within this process politics and the more local nationalistic concerns of government are also insecure as 'foreign capital' and 'exportation' define the means by which a sound and secure economy is created. The huge psychological collective changes identified by Samuels, to which politicians play little regard, are not simply disturbances that occur as part of the nature of social and economic change. Rather, they are indications of the damage being done to the social fabric and its modes of communication. They are evidence of 'collateral damage', that which has to be suffered for the 'collective good', and the achievement of specific competitive aims.

In the First World War this was called 'wastage'. This referred to the number of soldiers lost in order to achieve a given territorial gain (Shephard 2000). The majority of psychiatrists were complicit in both the language used and the means of ensuring that wastage from neurological disorder (shell-shock), did not detract from the wastage possible on the battlefield. My use of combative terms, the euphemisms of the military, is not misplaced in this context. Indeed, our understanding is always framed within the language used and the attitudes that language implies. It is a matter of what sort of communication takes place and what sort of reality that communication constructs.

As a general rule, an explanation of events that disempowers an individual or group is given precisely in order to create disempowerment. For empowerment to occur the explanation and the consequences have to be interpreted differently. The means to this lies in adopting a different form of communication. This, in turn, creates a different balance of power. In practice this amounts to an event synonymous with a declaration of war.

Communication in a cooling climate

To elaborate on the explanation of this state of affairs, Bauman is again useful. He speaks of the *"cooling off of the human planet"* (Bauman 1999: 53). By this he means that there is a cooling in human relations. This includes a *"coldness against 'foreigners in our midst'"* (op-cit). The use of these terms 'cooling' and 'coldness' are metaphorically very interesting. One reason why this is so again relates to the use of language. Such language as this is connotative in its imposition of meaning. This is at variance with denotative usage. The basis of difference relates to whether the terms used and the argument presented are represented as purely rational/analytic in design or employing, as all metaphoric use does, some larger affective purpose-in other words it makes implicit reference to the emotive. Cooling, for Bauman, refers to threat and danger, the beginnings of pathology in which we are apt to view the unfamiliar with suspicion rather than warmth. It is a resurgence of 'tribal hostility' (Bauman 1999: 55). Referring to Milan Kundera's reflections on laughter having a particular social character that epitomises a person's disposition in any context, he cites the ambivalence of laughter which reflects the condition of a society and the dispositions of individuals within it. This play on laughter he, following Kundera, regards as 'semantic imposture' (Bauman 1999: 56). It can express the sentiment of, and affirmation of, the angelic, joyful and inclusive (spiritual) rightness of a certain order of things, or a devilish aping of this same sound: an apparent affirmation of the same but, nonetheless, a hollow mimicry that has the intention to despoil the same. We think of laughter as a warm form of communication, but it can be a cold one, 'laughing at', or just a pretence.

Departing somewhat from Bauman's analogy I wish to suggest that the coldness of the second form of laughter is cynically present in the relational structures of communication erected by the economics of our age, driven by free-market exploitation. Following Bauman, I suggest this has resulted in a tribalism based on inclusion or exclusion in relation to our economic potential. It is, we might claim, a spiritually bereft, amoral laughter that we experience that is based on finding a security against the insecure: migrants, the unemployed and criminals in particular. In public measures it manifests itself in ever-increasing regulation that defends those included in the wealthy tribe. This is made possible by such measures as the privatisation of security and public space becoming private space: the development of 'colonies' (guarded estates), for example, or malls owned by private companies with security guards. Bauman quotes a report in the *International Herald Tribune* of 17 November 1997 as indicative of the relational coldness he identifies. Twenty-two-year-old Suzanne Lazare, who had settled in Denmark from Trinidad twelve years earlier, said she was thinking of leaving Denmark because *"Their eyes have changed...The Danes look down on you now. People are becoming very cold...Funny thing, it's towards themselves too"* (Bauman 1999: 52-53).

Peter Hoeg points to something similar in *Miss Smilla's Feeling for Snow*, in dwelling on the subject of silence. The title character, a Greenlander in Denmark, muses in an interview: *"I sit there in total silence. It's always interesting to leave Europeans in silence. For them it's a vacuum in which the tension grows and converges towards the intolerable"* (Hoeg 1996: 17). Silence too, then, has the potential to cool the climate of relationships. Here it is used to create discomfort for one who presumes themselves superior - the sense offered being that the superiority of the European is communicated in the way in which they relate through their language. The observation, however, can be turned around. The silence of the powerful can also act as a barrier to communication, but leaving the one who seeks answers in a hopeless vacuum of identity, rather than just with a sense of social discomfort. This authoratorial, bureaucratic silence, the silence that silences, is something that not only Europeans, but specifically bureaucrats and entrepreneurial capitalists, are actually quite good at.

The way we look at people falls into the same category of unspoken attitudes and relationship. It can be cold or warm, suggest power or concern. These unspoken forms of communication are far more immediate and telling than spoken ones that may follow them. In our relationships with our children they are the first language learnt. And, within schools, they are the first indication of the health or otherwise of the school community.

The look, laughter and silence reflect the dispositions of individuals in a society and become an expression of the social climate and its values. They can all become aspects of the gaze, as understood by Foucault (Foucault 1991), the means of social exclusion and inclusion, identification and control, within a climate of suspicion and competition. To extrapolate further from Bauman's metaphor of climate we may say that coldness or warmth are brought about by climatic conditions that work together to determine the overall environment. I am using this analogously to suggest that in the social sphere there always exists a political and economic climate within which relations work and of which those relations are themselves an expression. Laughter, the look, silence and other modes of expression are located within a pervading political-spiritual 'grammar' or consensus of attitudes. They are not just a sign of specific relations between specific individuals. Once this is understood we cannot pretend that our ability to relate to one another can be approached educationally without attention being paid to the political climate framing and suffusing relations. To do so would be to create a code of values that breaks down every time it is challenged by that climate, i.e., once there is a politico-social price to pay. Thus, there is a lip service paid to 'warmth', as far as values and relationships are concerned, which, since it has no political context, disappears when that political climate impinges.

Educationally, therefore, the climate is not mentioned. The values are preached or explored in the sterile and irrelevant isolation of the classroom without reference to the social reality in which they are to be employed.

This is not an educational omission, it is a political imposition. We might say, therefore, that in the politically suffused social domain values are connoted through these oblique references of style and tone by putting affective communication to use rather than by using the direct denotative communication of words as values statements. In this way what is addressed and imparted is the value of the spiritual identity of subjects in the social realm. In schools we pretend otherwise by speaking of unsituated moral codes. These are not unsituated because we do not apply them to specific, if imaginary, situations but because they are divorced from any political context, in which the complexity renders the insufficiency obvious.

By drawing attention to the way in which power is exercised within these cultural and social exchanges, I am also attempting to provide a complementary illustration of a theme central to Edward Said's work. This is commented upon by Liam Gearon: *"Said's abiding theme is that the definition of the other is crucial to enhancing a sense of superiority and that this can be done in subtle, unsuspecting and unobvious ways"* (Gearon 2001: 100).

In this manner the spirit of an age is constructed. It imbues all institutional and social behaviour, denigrating dissent both formally in institutional structures and informally in the codes of communication. Thus, in our late-capitalist free-market economy in which the individual must demonstrate employability and those who are unemployed are not deserving because they fail to take advantage of opportunity, education changes to both reflect and promote these values. And, the form of social communication, of the indirect kind that I exemplified above, is also imbued with them. Values education is necessarily reduced to the inculcation of a normative code of conduct. Moral and Spiritual education is reduced to apolitical notions of care, concern, charity and appreciation of the natural world. This takes place on the unstated basis that we are the rightful, if competitively challenged, inheritors of prosperity and correct social values. Teachers and parents may wish to be caring and loving, but just the very busyness of a society which elevates progress, wealth and competition above all else, creates a sea-change in attitudes based on priorities in relation to time available. Professional duties have to be cost effective, time-efficient, and above all managed. Relationships are regulated by these imposed concerns. Possibilities are eliminated by them. In capitalist society 'time' is always a scarce commodity because there is never enough time to do what 'needs' to be done. There is never enough time because there is never enough wealth. This applies to education, because education, and specifically schooling, serves the capitalist ambition. It is in schools that the 'foot soldiers' of capitalism are trained and skilled.

Foucault and the idea of 'political spiritualité'

Foucault's analysis of knowledge is salient at this point. His use of the term 'archaeology' (this term is related to what I referred to at the beginning of this study as exhumation of a buried past), was about uncovering the function of communication and rules of a given period and why they are given legitimation (Carrette 2000: 11; Foucault 1969: 117). This we can understand in terms of how we come to speak and think within the values of a given political period (as explained in chapter two). One of the results of this analysis was to expose assumptions (Carrette 2000: 11), which determine the prescription of historical rules as though they were necessary and natural. A second result was the understanding that this overlays, or silences, difference. 'Archaeology', according to Foucault, is taking 'difference seriously' (Carrette 2000: 11; Foucault 1969: 170).

It is precisely this difference that marks out our spirituality, our sense of identity and values. Thus, it can be said, to silence difference is to silence our sense of the spiritual or our sense of identity. This is what it means to live in a 'cold climate'. And the reason for the coldness is understood once we realise how it is created by the overlaying of an imposition of rules relating to our common unity and purpose which erases the possibility of the expression of difference. Spiritual identity is the 'space they left blank' (Carrette 2000: 16; Foucault, 1966: 207), overlaid with a language of normality and consensus to prevent the observation of what is missing. This can be connected to what Samuels earlier referred to as the denial of the secret life or the political soul.

For Foucault the question of political spirituality is closely related to that of 'governmentality' and 'new relations of power' (Carrette 2000: 136). In this he was seeking to ascertain the relationship between subjectivity, spirituality and the political will. In his analysis of the 1978 Iranian Revolution he writes that Shi'a Islam provided the Iranian people with, *"the promise and guarantee of finding something that would radically change their subjectivity'* and he is intrigued by how *'the spiritual...mobilizes a 'political will'"* (Carrette 2000: 137). What the Iranian Revolution did, and what interested Foucault as a result, was challenge the government of the Shah and mobilise the political will by thinking differently, at a fundamental level, as to the nature of the political reality. It did this by recognising that there was a spiritual void, a lack of meaningful identity and difference that constituted being Iranian. This lead Foucault to reflect as follows:

"How can one analyze the connection between ways of distinguishing true and false and ways of governing oneself and others? The search for a new foundation for each of these practices, in itself and relative to the other, the will to discover a different way of governing

oneself through a different way of dividing up true and false-this is what I would call 'political spiritualite'".
(Carrette 2000: 137; Foucault 1978: 82)

I think this is the level at which we have to apply ourselves if we wish to overcome the oppressive and impoverishing spiritual vacuum in which we find ourselves politically and educationally. It provides a way of recovering the tradition of dissent that has been exorcised within our present political and educational climate. It is a means to recognising that the norms and rules which presently apply are just that-imposed notions of true and false.

Here we can find a basis for identifying a different sense of educational purpose. The spiritual, states Foucault *"...involves a transformation of the subject"*. Instead of *"acceding to a certain mode of being"*, that is, being controlled by the power relations that are imposed by government and corporate capitalism, which are presented as an objective reality and thus a necessity, we can recognise that these are enforced on us as a form of education. For Foucault, the political 'truth' is produced through 'multiple forms of constraint' applied by government (and the sense that it is necessary to be governed, by whatever agency). In effect, this amounts to believing that you need to be told what to do, think and feel. Foucault proposes that government and truth are bound together in a single process within which the political, ethical and spiritual are interwoven and form the *"mechanisms, techniques and procedures in the production of truth"* (Carrette 2000: 138; Bernauer and Mahon 1994: 147-154).

For Foucault, this means that a 'technology of power' is always at work, which attempts to order and categorise human life (Carrette 2000: 139). It follows, Carrette concludes from Foucault, that the spiritual *"becomes a form of power in the attempt to win territory in the governance of human life"* (Carrette 2000: 141). In relation to education we can recognise this technology of power operating in the changes it has undergone in what Paul Yeats has called its 'bureaucratization' (Yeats 1999, 2001). Within the documentation and procedures of consultation and consensus, produced by the government agencies (TTA, QCA, Ofsted), we can chart the manoeuvres employed to bring about a new educational mentality. Within this we can identify the strategies, classifications and compartment-alisations of specific aspects of education by the application of the small aims of standards and competencies. Teachers are required to 'train' students and are being 'trained' themselves to do this. The implications of 'training' reside in the recognition that it prohibits an awareness of analyses such as that of Foucault, above.

We are not meant to be aware of the over-arching political conceptualisation of the system within which we are working. We are meant to believe in its efficacy and attend to those problems that arise within it, not by reflecting critically on whether it is an appropriate conception of education, but by regarding such problems as ones that simply require more time to solve.

The educational issue here is that 'training' is a conception of education that will ensure we will lack the necessary education to question and articulate a critique of the system itself. Such a critique requires an education that criticises 'education', not a system within which 'providers' wait for the next handout of instructions, submit plans for implementation to gain both money and approval, and then prepare for the next round of inspection.

All of this is subjected to the scrutiny of those with the official title of bureaucrats not educationalists. Within a generation we might expect that the lexicon of educational language would completely erase the conception of education that I am articulating. Unless we recognise that, contrary to our present experience, power can be exercised from innumerable points and we possess a form of power in the notion of a political spirituality. This relates to our forgotten democratic history. This power resides in the type and purpose of our forms of communication and the will that motivates us in the face of derision and detraction: the look, the silence and the laughter.

References Chapter 3

Bauman, Z. (1999) *In Search of Politics*, Cambridge: Polity Press.

Bernauer and Mahon (1994) 'The Ethics of Michel Foucault' in *Foucault: The Cambridge Companion*, Gutting, G. (ed.), Cambridge: Cambridge University Press. pp.141-58.

Carrette, Jeremy R. (2000) *Foucault and Religion: Spiritual Corporality and Political Spirituality*, London and New York: Routledge.

Foucault M. (1978) 'Questions of Method' in *The Foucault Effect: Studies in Governmentality*, Graham Burchell, Colin Gordon and Peter Miller (eds.), Hemel Hempstead: Harvester Wheatsheaf. pp.73-86.

Foucault, M.(1966) *The Order of Things: An Archeology of the Human Sciences*, London: Routledge.

Foucault, M. (1991) *Discipline and Punish: the birth of the prison*, London, Penguin.

Foucault, Michel (1969) *The Archaeology of Knowledge*, London: Routledge.

Gearon, Liam (2001) 'The Imagined Other: Postcolonial Theory and Religious Education', *British Journal of Religious Education* 23:2. pp.98-106.

Hoeg, Peter (1996) *Miss Smilla's Feeling for Snow*, London: The Harvill Press.

Samuels, A. (2001) *Politics on the Couch: Citizenship and the Internal Life*, London: Profile Books.

Shephard, Ben (2000) *A War of Nerves: Soldiers and Psychiatrists 1914-1994*, London: Jonathan Cape.

Yeats P. (1999) 'The Bureaucratization of Spirituality', *The International Journal of Children's Spirituality*, 4: 2. pp.179-194.

Yeats, Paul (2001) 'Postmodernism, Spirituality and Education in Late Modernity', in Jane Erricker, Cathy Ota and Clive Erricker (eds.), *Spiritual Education: Cultural, Religious and Social Differences, New Perspectives for the 21st Century*, Brighton: Sussex Academic Press

Chapter four

The school: prison house of impoverished expectation

Why should I claim that the school is a place of impoverished expectation? Despite claims to the contrary, that insist that the school is a place of opportunity for learners, it is not. The children are there for the teacher, the teacher is there to carry out the requirements of the centralised agencies, the centralised agencies are there to implement government policy, government policy aims to create wealth. The schools and the children are there to serve the government in this aim, everything else is subservient to this.

So far, I have dwelt on the economic and political issues that afflict education and presented the notion of a political spirituality that can provide a renewed and alternative vision. In this chapter, I wish to conclude by identifying the problematic role of the school, and how that can be analysed as a social institution that promotes competition and insecurity rather than fairness and equity. My argument is that through regulation, our schooling system is designed to produce consumers who have sufficient skills to earn the wealth for their desired consumption. This desire is fuelled by the economic system in which they are nurtured. The values questions that this system raises are ignored.

The economics of desire

Peter Donaldson outlined the basic characteristics and difficulties that beset economies in his book *Economics of the Real World.* At the end of his first chapter he summarises his argument:

> *"...the so-called 'ends' of economic policy - full employment, rapid economic growth, balance of payments equilibrium and price stability - are nothing of the sort. They are means rather than ends - and it is ends which concern ordinary people. What makes economics seem unreal and remote from them is the fact that it never seems directed to matters which are of urgent importance in their everyday lives...Above all, perhaps, we are concerned with the issue of equity - whether or not the economic system is working* fairly. *The distribution of income and wealth, how much we get and have compared with others, occupies a central place in most people's thoughts about economics...This is the stuff of the real world."*   (ibid: 21)

I think Donaldson is right that this does concern us. But, I am not sure that the notion of equity has remained the standard by which an economy is judged in the intervening period since he was writing. In pointing out the two different approaches to economics, he speaks of the Command Economy, which seeks to provide those goods and services which consumers need or ought to want and the Market Economy, in which the 'factors of production', land, labour and capital, are offered for sale and consumers buy accordingly. Thus, the latter relies on consumer demand without any state intervention. We exist today in the second system. The possibilities of wants that are unlimited, within this system, as far as the consumer is concerned, however, mitigates against the issue of equity. The unregulated free market has no concern with equity but only with increasing consumer demand. The effect on the consumer is to exacerbate the notion of wants further beyond the notion of needs. Such a volatile situation, given, as Donaldson states, that *"resources at any given time are strictly limited in supply"* and that *"the more resources that are used for one particular form of output, the less there are available for others"* (Ibid: 21), diminishes the concern for equity except insofar as I feel I am losing out. For those in this system who do well the financial reward is sufficient. Such a system defends itself on the basis of 'consumer choice', it is giving people what they want. But 'people' is a general and inclusive term that cannot apply evenly within an economy that creates wealth inequality. Increasingly, it provides for the prosperous, thus, over and above the basic needs we all have, it seeks to create a market for the consumption of the prosperous: a market of luxuries. This also preys upon the idea of providing, in material form, that which satisfies non-material (which we might call 'spiritual') needs. The duplicity with which wants are advertised as needs is part of the management of desire that corporatism seeks to control.

The market economy is based on desires or wants, not needs, and is about self-serving. Branding is about getting people to want something as if they need it. Thus it is a commodification of the idea of identity, image and lifestyle not just the sale of specific goods. The desire here is not just for the object, but for its symbolic value in relation to 'self'. It is based on how I feel about myself in relation to how others see me. Thus, despite the sales pitch regarding the satisfaction of desire (you can be who you want to be), it is simply another form of conformism, normalising, and regulation.

Desire breeds desire simply because it is not fixed on any particular thing but the thrill of desiring, whether it be sex, status, image, etc., and the sense of inadequacy that accompanies it. Being enslaved by desire is just one type of addiction that can be stimulated and preyed upon by the legitimated, corporate equivalent of the drug dealer or pimp. Within the psychology of desire our mentality takes no account of the needs of others. Their otherness, in so far as their needs impinging upon our consciousness, is based on the disturbance caused to our desiring state. Effectively, what we witness in these images of otherness is our own brutality: here are the victims or losers in the fiercely competitive wealth creation of the free market. What has been created is an insatiable desire for 'identity' through the acquisition of particular things. It is the idea that *things* confer identity, rather than relationships, that ensures the perpetuation of the free market economy.

There is even the option for us to do penance, to salve our conscience despite the fact that we are aware of the inequality such a system creates. That is what constitutes the idea of charity. The *idea* of charity to the world of the free market cannot be over-estimated, it is as important as penance was to the hierarchical churches. It forms part of the 'governmentality' involved. But acts of charity are purely symbolic in that they do not affect the brutality of the system. They merely provide some relief from its oppressiveness. To assuage our guilt we are presented with ways of giving and examples of the fruits of our giving. The *Children in Need Campaign* is a foremost example of this: we are *'entertained' to give* as well as entreated to give. This helps us to believe that the balance between our desires and others needs is appropriately adjusted. We have contributed to *fairness* in some form. The very fact that *we have chosen* to do this underlines the unfairness of such an idea.

The function of the school

Desire is intrinsically necessary for the free market economy system to succeed, therefore desire must be instilled into us. Where better to do this than in those institutions established for the nurture of the young: schools. But, for the production of desire, there needs to be, ironically, the imposition of discipline.

Foucault relates discipline, as conceived of in a disciplinary society, to schools in the following way. The order of discipline is an artificial order. It is related to the idea of the time required to complete a particular exercise which, therefore, prescribes a regularity, or norm, that is also a rule, which, in turn, presumes a level of aptitude. When speaking of the Christian Schools, he is referring at this point to French schools in the late eighteenth century, the understanding was that the pupils should never be placed in a lesson of which they were not yet capable. But, because there was a duration to each fixed stage of learning pupils who had not sufficiently progressed during that stage were placed on the bench of the 'ignorant' (Foucault 1991: 179). In relation to punishment he cites La Salle:

> *"By the word punishment, one must understand everything that is capable of making children feel the offence they have committed, everything that is capable of humiliating them, of confusing them: a certain coldness, a certain indifference, a question, a humiliation, a removal from office."*
> (La Salle 1783: 204-5; ibid: 178)

Here we are reminded of Bauman's reference to the look, laughter and the reference to silence, in chapter two. But surely, here we are identifying historical attitudes of two centuries ago. Not exactly, methods may have changed to some extent but the framework of understanding remains. Foucault is concerned with the underlying principle of 'normalizing judgement' of disciplinary technique (ibid: 183). He points out in his study that the means of punishment and discipline may change across time, but that is not equivalent to the system changing, only the method by which it is imposed. What changes is the mechanism of operation. The school today divides up time just as rigorously, into curriculum time. There is a hierarchy of disciplines, with Maths and English pre-eminent, along with Science and, the newly established Information Communication Technology (ICT). In primary schools this suffices apart from smaller doses of other humanities subjects and physical education. In teacher training degrees the creative arts have all but disappeared within the system of 'training' and specialisms at my own university, on these courses, no longer include them or the humanities subjects.

Thus, the notion of discipline, the incarceration of learning in specific disciplines, within the specifics of the curriculum day is the foundation of learning in schools. This is regulated also, in relation to attainment, across time: lessons, schemes of work, years and key stages, by assessments and tests (SATS). As a result the progression and achievement of pupils is 'measured' and reported. This is how they are judged, and the judicial metaphor is apt since, as Foucault remarks:

> *"within a homogeneity that is the rule, the norm induces, as a useful imperative and as a result of measurement, all the shading of individual differences... The examination combines the techniques of an observing hierarchy and those of a normalizing judgement. It is a normalizing gaze, a surveillance that makes it possible to qualify, to classify and to punish. It establishes over individuals a visibility through which one differentiates them and judges them."* (Ibid: 184)

Thus, the school becomes an equivalent of the prison, just as for Edmond Holmes it was a museum. For those who are successful within it this appears not to be the case. For those who are unsuccessful this is apparent. But, for all, the school is a prison-house of specific expectations and not just in relation to academic achievement. Schools instil values and, at first sight, these values appear uncontroversial until we recognise that they too are about normalisation. Fairness, sensitivity, concern for others, appreciating the natural world and other species, not stealing or lying; these all appear to be appropriate messages to be giving to children and appropriate ways of judging their conduct. But, the practical reality is far more messy and thus, as a result, its normalisation is demanded.

The desire that is inculcated in the school is that of academic achievement and social conformity. Academic achievement is the means of access to a higher position in a hierarchical society, which will confer status and wealth. It will also confer security, which we turn to later below. Social conformity is necessary in order to take advantage of academic achievement; from the wearing of the suit, or uniform, to the espousal of specific values, couched in their appropriate language of concern and restraint.

This, of course, does not prevent the very rich from behaviours such as tax-evasion by means of utilising 'legitimating' measures, such as offshore banking or property ownership. These mitigate against any sense of fairness (see Evans and Hencke 2002: 4-5). Beneficiaries of this system include Margaret Thatcher and Mohamed Al Fayed. It seems then, that these values to be inculcated in schools, largely function as a means to ensuring that those who do not benefit from the system do not act against it and that those who achieve to some degree know their place. At a certain point of wealth accumulation, the rules can be legitimately bent such that self-serving is promoted over and above the values one is *meant* to espouse. Importantly, one is not meant to ask questions about this. Lady Thatcher's office replied, 'No one's going to tell you about that.' And another respondent declined comment on the basis that, 'It is private.' Thus, it seems, we have private values for those who succeed in the private sector and public values that are applied to those who we might call 'the public'. The important point to note, in relation to academic achievement, which is discussed further below, is that pupils who are high achievers in school recognise that this is a passport into that private realm of wealth creation. At the other end of the scale, low achievers realise that, if they cannot succeed by this route, they must resort to alternative values to create their wealth within a non-legitimised system of operation.

But, one can argue that exercising social control is not what most teachers perceive themselves to be doing in schools, and the majority of committed teachers probably have the welfare of their children and young people in mind. That is not the point. Prison warders can have the welfare of their prisoners in mind and be consciously working toward their charges' rehabilitation. But they do so within the prison system, within the limits of encarceration. In fact, the regime of the benign prison follows quite closely that of the school day. And parents' evenings which take place in the main school hall bear marked formal resemblance to visiting times in prisons.

The values within the school act as a form of social control that works well for those who conform and succeed but pushes those who do not into situations of docile acceptance, punishment or even exclusion. Where the critical mass is high enough control within starts to break down. This critical mass is generated by the location of the school, and its type or character (for example, church schools on the one hand and what are termed 'sink' schools on the other) and the desire of parents to live in the locality of a particular type of school. The cost of housing in the area of a favoured school, which is succeeding in the system, will generally be higher. Thus, income becomes a crucial factor in educational achievement. This ensures educational success will be harder to achieve in other schools with poorer catchment areas. Thus, schooling replicates the effects of the free-market economy, even if a system of parental choice is not operated. When it is, the problem is greater because it is usually accompanied by a system of selection.

The regulation introduced to purportedly deal with the problem of lack of achievement: inspection, failing schools, league tables, exclusion of pupils and special measures actually contribute to it. Ostensibly about raising achievement, it highlights failure and resorts to the measures of punishment. The idea that a school is failing its pupils depends upon a specific notion of achievement that bears no relation to the needs and requirements of pupils in schools where the intake is different in terms of class, income, family stability and home and community values. It is a classic case of treating the symptoms but not the cause. It is also a good example of increasing surveillance, which is an idea central to Foucault's critique in his use of the metaphor of panopticism, taken from Jeremy Bentham's innovation of the panopticon: a tower to be used in prisons and other institutions requiring surveillance.

> *"Whenever one is dealing with a multiplicity of individuals on whom a task or a particular form of behaviour must be imposed, the panoptic schema may be used. It is - necessary modifications apart - applicable 'to all establishments whatsoever, in which, within a space not too large to be covered or commanded by buildings, a number of persons are meant to be kept under inspection'...In each of its applications, it makes it possible to perfect the exercise of power."*
> (Foucault 1991: 205-6; quoting Bentham 1843: 40)

Panopticism, as Foucault uses the term, identifies that such surveillance no longer relies upon a literal space and can be applied in all institutional contexts to enforce control as an instrument of power.

Academic achievement in schools is measured by differing forms of assessment but principally by examinations. This is also largely the case in the majority of higher education institutions. Why should this be the case and what is the relevance of examinations to students' capacity to achieve? Bourdieu and Passeron's analysis of this is interesting. Although their study is focused on the French higher education system much of it is directly applicable to our own. Here I both summarise and adapt their argument and comment upon it.

In schools, and in higher education, the design of the system will be in the interests of those who have benefited from it. The notion of success will be according to their criteria. The system of grading must distinguish the relative ability of all students and the award will be an official summation of this graded ability. By this means 'the power of transmitting power from one generation to another' exists as an apparently neutral authority. *"But through its formally irreproachable verdicts, which always objectively serve the dominant classes...the School is better able than ever...to contribute to the reproduction of the established order, since it succeeds better than ever in concealing the function it performs"* because, at the same time, it gives credibility to the idea of social mobility and individual opportunity: the examination is the same for all, the education given in the institution or across institutions, is the same for all. Everything is regulated to ensure standards and opportunity. The school is a liberating force, there for the individual to use to his or her own advantage (see Bourdieu P. and Passeron J-C. 1990: 167).

In summary, the school and the university are there for the success of those who can succeed according to those institutions' criteria of success. The purpose is to create a stratified ranking, it is not a by-product of the system, which then advertises the comparative worth of each individual to the employer and society. For those who find this system difficult academically, as they progress to higher studies and increasing academic expectations such as A levels, but who, in middle class terms according to parental expectation, are expected to enter higher education, and, in terms of diligence have faithfully attempted to succeed but with moderate success due to limited intellectual interest or acumen, we offer professional status within the teaching profession. Arguably, the majority of primary and a good percentage of secondary teachers probably fit this description. Though there are, certainly, exceptions to this within our system of employment opportunities. Following on from our educational framework, as described above, those who enter the teaching profession are then duty bound to perpetuate the system in place. Their mortgages depend upon it. What they then do is what was done to them.

> *"Pedagogic work...has the effect of producing individuals durably and systematically modified...to endow them...with common schemes of thought, perception, appreciation and action...i.e. agents capable of exerting a transformative action reproductive of the training they themselves received."*
> (Ibid: 196)

This is ensured through the surveillance techniques described above which, in teacher training institutions, means the government tells the institution what must be taught and the standards to achieve, the student requires the institution and its lecturers to tell him or her how to do it. The student then replicates this accomplishment in school and is judged by the results his or her children achieve.

The reason for the importance of achievement goes beyond academic criteria. It is not being educated in subjects that matters but the acquisition of specific skills and attitudes. Why is this so? Because the achievement gained translates directly into the economy. In the relationship between first and third world, the problems in the third world lie in needing to raise the skills of their populous to challenge first world economic dominance. Equally, for the first world the issue is to increase the capacity of the workforce to sustain dominance. Also, since consumer spending is so important to the survival of capitalist interests, it is important to school the young into a system of consumerism with the capacity to spend due to their level of income. It is in the interest of capitalist societies to create skilled consumers to establish a wealthy nation-state. The threat exists that corporations might find better markets elsewhere if another country's economy provides this possibility. Therefore, in principle, the third world is no longer necessarily specifically geographically located; whilst, at the moment, Asian countries provide the lowest paid work force in a de-regulated health and safety environment, that could be transferred if market economies change in status.

The third world is coming home. Just as Manchester provided impoverished conditions for its industrial workforce, attested to by Engels, in the 19th century, so it is possible in the 21st. The western nation state survives or perishes economically according to its ability to conform its present and future citizens to an education that serves capitalist interest and a consumer mentality that desires what capital produces. Because not all citizens can achieve what is required to sustain this process, except in a basic fashion as factory workers and manual labourers, they are our contribution to the third world. Once this is realised the result is social unrest and ghettoised mentalities of those who know they do not belong to mainstream society and are excluded. We have already witnessed examples of this in Bradford, Burnley, Brixton and elsewhere. The Damilolo Taylor affair relates this phenomenon to an established acceptance of crime, lawlessness and the impossibility of managing schools, policing, or housing environments in such areas. As we noted in chapter 1, there is a fire underground, but it is not just 'elsewhere'.

The insecurity of the free-market

Where insecurity exists the desire to create security increases, but it is a desire that can only be satisfied by economic wealth, given our lack of the preservation of community. Zygmunt Bauman dwells on these themes in *Community: seeking safety in an insecure world.* In his last chapter he makes observations on the ghetto. He speaks of the increased value of place in a society in which insecurity has been fostered by

> *"the new global network of dependencies combined with the relentless dismantling of the institutional safety-net which used to protect us from the vagaries of the market and the caprices of a market concocted fate."* (Ibid: 110-1)

The abstraction of 'society' is not enough to create a sense of belonging. We are told that there is a need for 'flexibility' in relation to employment and location and it is the individuals responsibility to respond to this in advertising their skills. Individuals are admonished to

> *"exercise their own wits in the search for survival, improvement and a dignified life, to rely on their own guts and stamina and blame their lassitude or laziness in the event that they suffer defeat."* (Ibid: 112)

Within this state of insecurity both rich and poor need to find their own sense of community, in some tangible and localised form. The rich achieve it through fortressing themselves in their 'colonies'. Here the term for places of penal servitude is transmuted into the idea of a safe place because it is fully privatised: locked gates with digital codes keep non-residents out, signs stating 'armed response' in gardens indicate to any would-be trespasser and transgressor that there is a private service that will penalise any invasion with weaponry. The rest, says Bauman, *"can do next to nothing to mitigate the uncertainty and insecurity in the world they inhabit"* (ibid: 113). Whereas 'community' used to refer to a place of safety and belonging achieved through trust, mutual benefit and relational dependence now it stands for *"isolation, separation and guarded gates"* (ibid: 114).

We must guard against idealising the idea of community. In practice, specific communities are always preserving something in common against the other, the stranger whose values and behaviours are different. But when the preservation of community is insecure then, rather than communities safeguarding what they positively value, 'communities' are constructed negatively, according to what has to be rejected or repressed.

Schools, as forms of community and serving local communities, can operate according to either model, but they will decide in relation to the perception of security or insecurity they enjoy. Inevitably, schools within localities that present them with greater threat of insecurity will be more repressive and punitive: exclusion and punitive measures will be introduced to safeguard values and behaviour. In schools within a location where the threat is less apparent a more benign and tolerant regime will operate (within the gates). Here we can observe the replication, within institutionalised education, of Bauman's observations with regard to community and society in general. Ghettoising within society creates ghetto schools. This process may be more complex than the analysis so far has suggested. It may be cumulative according to a number of factors.

We have already mentioned the distinctions in school community relating to catchment areas. This is a difference based on class and income. There is also the emergence of faith schools. Church of England schools have traditionally tended to attract middle class parents who wish their children to go to them for values rather than just faith reasons-thus this tends to be a class issue rather than just a faith issue. But, the new initiative to create more faith schools across a number of religions presents a different situation. Jewish schools and Roman Catholic schools have been established for a considerable period of time. They vary to the extent that they are attempting to preserve a faith identity and/or a class one, but the faith issue is more dominant. With newer Islamic, Hindu and other faith schools they again seek to inculcate faith values but can also be about seeking to develop opportunities for children with faith backgrounds within the economy.

Refugee children present a new challenge. David Blunkett's comment on not 'swamping' schools in particular locations with them and setting up a separate school for them suggests retaining some sort of 'purity' for the local state school until some sort of assimilation can be achieved into the norms and expectations of our schooling system. Independent, fee paying, schools (or preparatory and public schools) are the traditional way for parents to socialise their children into a bourgoise culture that rejects 'lower' social values and offers the possibility of greater opportunity. There are even 'alternative' independent schools such as Summerhill, Brockwood Park (the Krishnamurti Foundation) or the relatively newly established Buddhist Dhamma School in Brighton, that seek to operate according to alternative values. Whilst, benignly, these examples can be looked upon as simply representing diversity and choice, this is hardly the case. They are examples of attempts to escape from the alternative to choice-schools which fail children. The notion of failure will be perceived differently by different groups but in each case there will be two elements: failure in terms of academic achievement and failure in terms of values. No-one wants their child to go to a school full of refugees, nor do they want their child to go to a school with a high level of low-achievers. Thus we establish a second sort of refugee-colonies of low-achievers, schools that fail, an underclass, a different sort of ghetto.

In this kind of social environment, as Bauman observes, the call is for

> "*more government to mask and contain the deleterious social consequences, in the lower regions of social space, of the de-regulation of wage labour and the deterioration of social protection.*"   (Ibid: 121)

In this way market capitalism produces exactly the reverse of what the dissenting tradition called for. De-regulation of the economy produces insecurity, ghettos and the call for more regulation of society as a protection from the poor. It produces the absurdity of zero tolerance against crime without a thought for what causes crime. It produces 'schools that wish to do the best for their pupils', which introduce them to notions of citizenship education dwelling on issues of duty, rights, fairness and rules within a system of manifest inequality. This only works in schools where the possibility of opportunity exists for the pupils because the deceit that the system is both in their interests and fair can be maintained. In other schools, the pupils are already aware of the deceit and how it affects them. In neither type of school is learning in the interests of the pupil. In both what is being taught is conformity to a system that protects the rich and the powerful by producing an orderly society with citizens that want to be governed. At the same time the young are taught that they must compete with one another in order to earn the right to the share of capital that they deserve in adult life through the mode of employment they attain. This is a curious case of divide and rule which is branded as 'entreprenurial' education. Not conforming results in exclusion. From the English Civil War to the present, though society and education have been superficially transformed, beneath the surface nothing of significance has changed.

References for Chapter 4

Bauman, Z. (2001) *Community: seeking safety in an insecure world,* Cambridge: Polity.

Bentham, J. (1843), Bowring (ed.) *Works*, IV.

Bourdieu, P. and Passeron, J. C. (1990) *Reproduction in Education Society and Culture* 2nd edition, London: Sage.

Donaldson, Peter (1973) *Economics of the Real World*, Harmondsworth: Penguin.

Evans, Rob and Hencke, David (2002) 'Tax loopholes on homes benefit the rich and cost UK millions', London and Manchester: *The Guardian*, Saturday May 25.

Foucault, M. (1991) *Discipline and Punish: The Birth of the Prison*, Harmondsworth: Penguin.

La Salle, J. B. (1783) *Conduite des ecoles chretiennes,* B.N. MS. 11759. *Traite sur les obligations des freres des ecoles chretiennes.*

Conclusion

Our society is not served by, and our institutions are collapsing under, the weight of government regulation and the impetus to de-regulation in the economic world. What is happening in schools and higher education institutions is symptomatic of this. Proposals for widening access in higher education by ensuring that more working class and poor gain university education have resulted in nothing of the sort. The 'cohort studies' of 1958, 1970 and 2000 which track generational change in relation to parental incomes reveal that *"access to higher education is closely and increasingly linked to family backgrounds...(that) expanding higher education has been a wonderful thing for the middle classes...(and) the powerful effect of education, and especially higher education, on earnings...(and that) the overall proportion of undergraduates from non-manual homes is exactly the same"* (Wolf 2002: 18-19).

In *Bringing Home The Revolution: The Case for a British Republic* Jonathan Freedland compares the democratic processes of the United States, with its emphasis on rights and liberties, to those of the United Kingdom. In relation to education he presents some interesting figures and observations. Berating our lack of democracy, he identifies the rise of unelected and unaccountable quangos established by the Conservative government in the 1980s and early 90s which New Labour have seen fit to extend. Education has suffered its measure of these with the Qualifications and Curriculum Authority (QCA) and the Office for Standards in Education (Ofsted) counted among them. Here we have *"unelected bodies performing executive functions for the government...An entire new class has emerged, like the nomenklatura of the old Soviet Union"* (Freedland 1999: 91). This new surveillance mechanism, ensuring conformity and denying professional liberty and innovation costs, when the full range of quangos is taken account of, *"£20.84 billion of taxpayers' money"*. (ibid: 91). That is what we pay for our democratic rights to be removed and increased professional burdens to be placed on us. As parents, we may wish to restore these rights by educating our children at home. The major advantages of doing this lie in controlling the amount of pressure placed on your children, the values within which their development will occur and the relationship you can establish with them. In other words, both you and your children can exercise your democratic rights with a comparative lack of bureaucratic interference. Nevertheless, there are costs in terms of time and income. Also, there have to be prior benefits to consider doing this, in terms of one's own education and an income that can support such a venture. My point is: why should this be necessary when we already pay for institutions to serve us in this respect?

Freedland's homily to the United States is not a call that I can respond to. He passes over inequality too lightly, though his criticisms of the United Kingdom are well aimed. Reflecting on his book raises some important questions. There are some singular issues to resolve regarding equality and liberty. Criticism of some dissenters was voiced in this study by Walker in chapter 1. This he put down to an 'overstrained moderation', by which he meant a lack of dissenting zeal in relation to the status quo. This can be observed in the American model of today in which economic avarice can happily interfere with equality on the basis of not restraining individual rights. This Freedland is happy to overlook or regard, at worst, as an unfortunate by-product of an otherwise model system. I think not. It is simply the capitalist rich having no regard for a system that oppresses the poor. This is what happens when the de-regulation of corporate activity allows abuse of economic power and political influence. The regulation of schools and other state institutions also represents the abuse of power by government in seeking the gain of economic reward with scant attention paid to liberty, equality or democracy. I think there is a real sense in which, despite changes in constitutional rights and forms of government, little progress has been made regarding educational possibility. In my view this can be put down to what education, in every circumstance, seeks to achieve in relation to the *compliance* of its citizens to the governmental and values system it regards as appropriate. It is the system that comes first, the law that enforces it, education that inculcates it. Below this surface we face the rather more messy reality, which goes back a good distance, as the following report observes.

When William Cobbett asked a labourer, in the period following the Enclosures Act, which brought about the case of the Tolpuddle Martyrs,
"How do you live upon half a crown a week?"
He replied *"I don't live upon it"*.
"How do you live, then?" asked Cobbett.
He replied, *"I poach, it is better to be hanged than starve to death"* (Marlow 1985: 31).

I think there are several lessons to be gleaned from the observations made above and those put forward earlier in this study. First, politicians lie, the poor steal, the rich both lie and steal and children in schools are admonished to do neither. Second, that government and institutionalised education (as it has historically and presently been arranged), are both detrimental to human potential. Third, that globalisation, as it is being pursued, will result in little progress and more barbarism, the majority of which will be legitimated in order to castigate the needy and protect economic interests. What the middle classes think they have to gain from this I do not know. In the short-term, security in an increasingly insecure world, but in the longer term the hope depends on our children so, perhaps, we should acquaint them with the 'real' world in which they are living. To do so we may apply a principle from Tom Paine *"Men (sic) are born and always continue, free, and equal in respect of their rights"* (Philp 1995: 162). As Rousseau added: man is everywhere in chains. One of the links in these chains is our system of education.

One reason why this is the case, derives from a conception of education that is insufficient by design. I propose that the prime purpose of education is for it to be life-enhancing. It was Nietzsche who said that collecting facts in a quasi-scientific way was a sterile pursuit. Goethe, whom Nietzsche quoted, said *"I hate everything that merely instructs me without augmenting or directly invigorating my activity"* (de Botton: 112). De Botton draws on Nietzsche and Goethe in relation to his own experience as a tourist in travelling around Madrid. His guide book he finds insufferably instructive. He comments, *"The guide-book might have added 'and...there must be something wrong with the traveller who cannot agree'"* (ibid: 114). It is full of facts which do not appeal to enquiry, *"The information gave no hint as to how curiosity might arise"* (ibid: 122). We might surmise that it was a curriculum of information in 'knowing' Madrid. De Botton suggests an alternative outcome of his travels might be to *"return from our journeys with a collection of small, unfeted but life enhancing thoughts"* (ibid: 113). This sounds like a worthwhile educational endeavour. It might mean that young people own ideas from which they can act and create. It would create conviction and a will to purpose. It would help them travel and determine their own travelling in life, rather than be instructed in educational purpose that is mapped for them. It might, of course, create dissent. This is the fear of those who govern. Institutionally, education is not what it seems or purports itself to be. First and foremost it is based on control. Its great fear is that we might think and manage things for ourselves, in favour of the enhancement of our own lives: that we might measure and come to know things for our own purposes.

We pride ourselves on our education, yet it creates injustice and is partisan. It leads those who benefit from the system in place to elevate their own self-importance and denigrate those who prosper less well. This effect is a rule of our social system that reinforces the way education is governed. James Agee reflected on these themes of self-importance and justice in his important study of sharecropper tenant farmers in the Cotton Belt of the United States in 1936, in *Let Us Now Praise Famous Men:*

> *"Even what seem to us our present soundest and most final ideas of justice are noticeably cavalier and provincial and self-centered. What would we have to think of hogs who, having managed to secure justice among themselves, still and continuously and without the undertone of a thought to the contrary exploited every other creature and material of the planet, and who wore in their eyes, perfectly undisturbed by any secondary consideration, the high and holy light of science and religion."*
>
> (Agee and Evans 2001: 224)

We have to ask, *"Who are the hogs?"* and *"Why do we recognise their exploitation as justice and teach it as such to our children?"* As Agee observes, *"It is probably never really wise, or even necessary, or anything better than harmful, to educate a human being toward a good end by telling him lies"* (ibid: 225).

But lies, like beauty, lie in the gaze of the beholder. We must remember that our education system is designed to teach us how to observe or gaze on the world. To learn how to see it otherwise - to be critically aware and astute - and to confidently to voice what we observe, is something we must learn to do for ourselves. If we ask what prevents this happening, we can focus on the great capitalist deceit: that we can all be rich and deserve to be. This transmutation of the dissenting call to freedom into its equation with riches is cleverly expressed in every advertising slogan and image and every political speech we hear and see. You have a right to be rich! Here the naivete of the utopianism of dissent is used to prey upon our own naivete as capitalist citizens. You can be rich, you can be free, you can be different. Believe that and you can be fooled. Do not expect your education to stop you being fooled, it is part of the process.

References for Conclusion

Agee, James and Evans, Walker (2001) *Let Us Now Praise Famous Men*, London: Violette Editions.

de Botton, Alain (2002) *The Art of Travel*, London: Hamish Hamilton.

Freedland, Jonathan (1999) *Bringing Home The Revolution: The Case for a British Republic*, London: Fourth Estate.

Marlow, Joyce (1985) *The Tolpuddle Martyrs*, London: Grafton Books.

Philp, M. ed. (1995) *Thomas Paine: Rights of Man, Common Sense, and other political writings*, Oxford: Oxford University Press.

Wolf, Alison (2002) 'We're still skipping (working) class', London: THES May 24.

Bibliography

Agee, James and Evans, Walker (2001) *Let Us Now Praise Famous Men*, London: Violette Editions.

Barnard, H. (1961) *A History of English Education From 1760*, London: University of London Press.

Baudrillard, Jean (1968) *Le Systeme des Objets*, Paris: Denoel-Gonthier.

Bauman, Z. (1999) *In Search of Politics*, Cambridge: Polity Press.

Bauman, Z. (2001) *Community: seeking safety in an insecure world,* Cambridge: Polity.

Bell, Jeffrey (1992) *Populism and Elitism: Politics in the Age of Equality*, Washington D.C.: Regnery.

Benjamin, W. (1999) *The Arcades Project*, Cambridge, Mass. and London, England: The Belknap Press of Harvard University Press.

Bentham J. (1843), Bowring (ed.) *Works*, IV.

Bernauer and Mahon (1994) 'The Ethics of Michel Foucault' in *Foucault: The Cambridge Companion*, Gutting, G, (ed.), Cambridge: Cambridge University Press. pp.141-58.

Bourdieu, Pierre and Passeron, Jean-Claude (1990) *Reproduction in Education, Society and Culture,* 2nd edition, London: Sage.

Britten, Daniel (1998) 'Free to do as we're told', London: *The Observer Review*, 14 June.

Carrette, Jeremy R. (2000) *Foucault and Religion: Spiritual Corporality and Political Spirituality*, London and New York: Routledge.

Clarke, J. and Newman, J. (1992) 'Managing to Survive: Dilemas of Changing organisational Forms in the Public Sector', paper presented at Social Policy Association Conference, University of Nottingham, July.

Debord, Guy (1977) *The Society of the Spectacle*, Detroit: Black and Red.

de Botton, Alain (2002) *The Art of Travel*, London: Hamish Hamilton.

Donaldson, Peter (1973) *Economics of the Real World*, Harmondsworth: Penguin.

Engels, F. (1987) *The Conditions of the Working Class in England*, London: Penguin.

Erricker, C. (1998) 'Spiritual Confusion: a critique of current educational policy in England and Wales', *The International Journal of Children's Spirituality*, 3:1. pp.51-64.

Evans, Rob and Hencke, David (2002) 'Tax loopholes on homes benefit the rich and cost UK millions', London and Manchester: *The Guardian*, Saturday May 25.

Foucault, M. (1978) 'Questions of Method' in *The Foucault Effect: Studies in Governmentality*, Burchell, G. Gordon, C. and Miller, P. (eds.), Hemel Hempstead: Harvester Wheatsheaf. pp.73-86.

Foucault, M. (1966) *The Order of Things: An Archaeology of the Human Sciences*, London: Routledge.

Foucault, M. (1991) *Discipline and Punish: the Birth of the Prison*, London: Penguin.

Foucault, M. (1969) *The Archaeology of Knowledge*, London: Routledge.

Fourier, Charles (1928) *Nouveau Tableaux de Paris: Vol. 1*, Paris: publisher unknown.

Frank, T. (2001) *One Market Under God*, London: Secker and Warburg.

Freedland, Jonathan (1999) *Bringing Home The Revolution: The Case for a British Republic*, London: Fourth Estate.

Freire, P. (1972) *Pedagogy of the Oppressed*, Harmondsworth: Penguin.

Gearon, Liam (2001) 'The Imagined Other: Postcolonial Theory and Religious Education', *British Journal of Religious Education* 23:2. pp.98-106.

Gewirtz, S., Ball, S. J., Bowe, R. (1995) *Markets, Choice and Equity in Education*, Buckingham: Open University Press.

Giroux, Henry A. (1996) 'Towards a Postmodern Pedagogy', in Lawrence Cahoone (ed.) *From Modernism to Postmodernism: An Anthology,* Cambridge, Mass and Oxford: Blackwell. pp. 687-697

Hoeg, Peter (1996) *Miss Smilla's Feeling for Snow*, London: The Harvill Press.

Klein, Naomi (2000) *No Logo: taking aim at the brand bullies,* London: HarperCollins.

La Salle, J. B. (1783) *Conduite des ecoles chretiennes,* B.N. MS. 11759. *Traite sur les obligations des freres des ecole chretiennes.*

Lillo, (1731) *The History of George Barnwell, or, the London Merchant* (publisher unknown)

Marlow, Joyce (1985) *The Tolpuddle Martyrs,* London: Grafton Books.

Marx, Karl (1977) *Economic and Philosophic Manuscripts of 1844,* Moscow: Progress Publishers.

Monbiot, George (2000) *Captive State: the corporate takeover of Britain*, London: Macmillan.

Orwell, George (1949) *Nineteen Eighty-four*, London: Secker and Warburg.

Pendergrast, Mark (1994) *For God, Country and Coca-Cola*, London: Phoenix.

Philp, M. ed. (1995) *Thomas Paine: Rights of Man, Common Sense and Other Political Writings*, Oxford: Oxford University Press.

Plant, Sadie (1992) *The Most Radical Gesture: The Situationist International in a Postmodern Age*, London and New York: Routledge.

Rorty, James (1934) *Our Master's Voice*, New York: The John Day Company.

Rousseau, Jean-Jacques (1993) *Emile*, London: The Everyman Library.

Samuels, A. (2001) *Politics on the Couch: Citizenship and the Internal Life*, London: Profile Books.

Saul John R. (1997) *The Unconscious Civilization*, London: Penguin.

Shephard, Ben (2000) *A War of Nerves: Soldiers and Psychiatrists 1914-1994*, London: Jonathan Cape.

Shute, C. (1998) *Edmond Holmes and The Tragedy of Education*, Nottingham: Educational Heretics Press.

Smith, Adam (1937) *The Wealth of Nations,* New York: Random House.

Smith, Adam (1976) *The Theory of Moral Sentiments*,
Oxford: Clarendon Press.
Spanos, William V. (1993) *The End of Education*,
Minneapolis and London: University of Minnesota Press.
Thompson, E. P. (1968) *The Making of the Working Class*,
Harmondsworth: Penguin.
Wolf, Alison (2002) 'We're still skipping (working) class',
London: THES May 24.
Woodcock, G. (1963) *Anarchism*, Harmondsworth: Penguin.
Yeats P. (1999) 'The Bureaucratization of Spirituality',
International Journal of Children's Spirituality, 4:2. pp.179-
194.
Yeats, P. (2001) 'Postmodernism, Spirituality and Education
in Late Modernity', in Erricker, J., Ota, C. and Erricker,C.
(eds.), *Spiritual Education: Cultural, Religious and Social
Differences, New Perspectives for the 21st Century,*
Brighton: Sussex Academic Press.